The Origins of Japanese
Industrial Power

THE ORIGINS OF
JAPANESE INDUSTRIAL
POWER

Strategy, Institutions and
the Development of
Organisational Capability

Edited by

ETSUO ABE and ROBERT FITZGERALD

FRANK CASS • LONDON

330.952 0

10 OCT 1995

First published in 1995 in Great Britain by
FRANK CASS AND COMPANY LIMITED
Newbury House, 890–900 Eastern Avenue, London,
IG2 7HH, England

and in the United States of America by
FRANK CASS
c/o ISBS, Inc.
5602 N.E. Hassalo Street, Portland, Oregon 927213-3640

British Library Cataloguing in Publication Data

Origins of Japanese Industrial Power: Strategy, Institutions and the
Development of Organisational Capability. – (Studies in Business
History, ISSN 0959–2296)
    I. Abe, Etsuo   II. Fitzgerald, Robert   III. Series
    338.0952
    ISBN 0–7146–4623–7 (cased)
    ISBN 0–7146–4157–X (paper)

Library of Congress Cataloging in Publication Data

The origins of Japanese industrial power : strategy, institutions and
  the development of organisational capability / edited by Etsuo Abe
  and Robert Fitzgerald.
    p. cm.
    "This group of studies first appeared in a special issue of Business history,
v. 37, no. 2, April 1995" – T.p. verso.
    Includes bubliographical references.
    ISBN 0–7146–4623–7 (cased) ISBN 0–7146–4157–X (paper)
    1. Japan – Economic policy – 1945– 2. Industrial promotion – Japan.
    3. Production management – Japan. 4. Industrial management – Japan.
    5. Japan – Economic conditions – 1945– I. Abe, Etsuo, 1949–.
    II. Fitzgerald, Robert.
    HC462.9.069 1995
    330.952′04 – dc20   94–38512
Printed in Great Britain by Antony Rowe Ltd   CIP

This group of studies first appeared in a Special Issue of Business History,
Vol.XXXVII, No.2 (April 1995), [The Origins of Japanese Industrial Power:
Strategy, Institutions and the Development of Organisational Capability].

Contents

Abstracts

Japanese Economic Success: Timing, Culture, and Organisational Capability, *by Etsuo Abe and Robert Fitzgerald*

Japanese economic success has been built upon the establishment and development of key manufacturing sectors, and the perspectives of business history can especially reveal that complex interaction of companies, markets, business networks, and state which has over time created a globally competitive industrial system. Long-term economic growth was capped in the 1950s and 1960s by growth rates that were unprecedented in their scale and duration. Similarly, the process of industrial transformation accelerated in the years between 1918 and 1950, important developments finally coalescing during the post-war period into the so-termed 'Japanese industrial system'. Debates over the timing of economic development in Japan are intertwined with debates on the contribution of a pre-industrial national culture to business success. The historical record suggests that the acquisition of organisational capabilities within Japanese manufacturers has been shaped by the timing of the country's industrialisation and by its consequent development needs. The nature of Japanese management and Japan's industrial system, although influenced by cultural attributes, was shaped by organisational and economic objectives attuned to the circumstances of the country's industrialisation, and competitive advantage followed from the unavoidably nationally specific process by which potential was ultimately matched by capability.

The Role of Managerial Enterprise in Post-War Japan's Economic Growth: Focus on the 1950s, *by Hidemasa Morikawa*

In pre-war Japan, large-scale business enterprises tended to become managerial enterprises, but around 1930 this transformation was still in a stage of transition. Managerial enterprises developed rapidly due to the militarisation of the economy during the Second World War, and, after 1945, following the dissolution of the *zaibatsu* by the occupying US forces. The purge of businessmen that had co-operated with the military, and tax and land reforms which affected the wealthiest, were other contributory factors. Economic growth after 1950 assisted the development of managerial enterprise, just as managerial enterprise accelerated economic growth by facilitating investment and the expansion of business capability. The majority of post-war Japan's most important executives were promoted from within their companies. They were already acquainted with their workforces, especially their engineers, and fully understood their capabilities. This knowledge and the support they enjoyed amongst their employees were critical to the strategic decision-making that guided the investments that brought rapid growth, and, with these organisational assets, they won the confidence and support of banks, business allies, and government. It was those managerial enterprises controlled by salaried managers promoted from within and the emergence of new entrepreneurial enterprises which led Japan's post-war economic growth.

Kigyo Shudan: The Formation and Functions of Enterprise Groups, by Takeo Kikkawa

The enterprise groups, formed after the Second World War, and horizontally linking a number of associated companies, are widely accepted as a notable characteristic of the 'Japanese Industrial Management System'. The purpose of these groups, and therefore their particular contribution to industrial organisational capability, is rooted in the period of their development, the 1950s. Interlocking share ownership within the groups brought a sense of security, allowed managers to exercise control over their companies, and encouraged firms to plan in terms of long-term growth rather than short-term profits. Nevertheless, the objectives and advantages of inter-firm groupings altered over time, and these changes reflected developments in the Japanese economy and in the commercial and organisational needs of companies. This institutional arrangement has been a notable aspect of the Japanese industrial system, characteristically distinct from the Anglo-American economies and a contributor to competitive advantage and differential growth rates.

The Formation of Distribution *Keiretsu*: the Case of Matsushita Electric, by Masahiro Shimotani

The Japanese *keiretsu*, specifically vertically linked firms, have attracted global attention, and there is continuing dispute over their purpose. They act as close, long-term business relationships between large corporations and a number of selected smaller firms. They have been seen as rational effective systems, especially suited to the circumstances of Japan's industrialisation, and as a factor in its economic success. On the other hand, they have been criticised as closed systems that exclude potential competitors. *Keiretsu* are generally divided into production *keiretsu*, financial *keiretsu*, and distribution *keiretsu*. As a pioneer of distribution *keiretsu*, Matsushita (Panasonic) grew in Japan by securing the outlet of its products at 'appropriate' prices, and is now its nation's largest electronics manufacturer. Its distribution structure was founded in the 1930s, but the changes introduced in the 1950s finally brought it substantial commercial advantages, and encouraged rivals to form similar networks.

The Rise of the Mass Market and Modern Retailers in Japan, *by Mariko Tatsuki*

The Japanese distribution system was established in the mid-eighteenth century, when the current stratified structure of wholesalers, brokers or middle merchants, and retailers was already evident. As a result, the mass manufacturers of consumer goods, including electric appliances and automobiles, began to market their own products in the 1950s, the traditional distribution system being unsuited to their requirements. Supermarkets and discounters emerged in the following decade. They had to compete against small retailers and the chain stores owned by large manufacturers, and their share of total consumer sales was limited even in the 1970s. Because of its history and fact of rapid post-war growth, retailing and marketing in Japan has retained unique features.

The Evolution of the Financial System in Post-War Japan, *by Tetsuji Okazaki*

The Japanese financial system is regarded as a key factor behind Japan's remarkable post-war growth. The main bank arrangements, linking companies with a principal source of funds, and complementary institutional networks were complex and intricate, and underpinned industrial investment and expansion. In the 1950s, the city banks, as the main banks of manufacturers, were asked to supply large amounts of funds to their clients, acting as substitutes of the stock market. As their liquidity decreased, post-war reconstruction policies reduced their risk-bearing capabilities. In order to stabilise the system and to sustain the funds needed for strategic industries, the Ministry of Finance and the Bank of Japan began actively to regulate the financial markets, while the Ministry of International Trade and Industry co-ordinated policy with the industrial sector. It was this system of complementary institutions, including the main banks, long-term financial institutions, and government agencies, which enabled Japan's high-speed growth.

The Development of Production Management at the Toyota Motor Corporation, *by Masaru Udagawa*

During the oil crisis of the early 1970s, which so damaged the international automobile industry, Japanese manufacturers were able to enlarge their share of world markets. Their advantage had been created over a long period, led by the Toyota Motor Corporation, and soon followed by competitors like Nissan. Creative production systems and quality control programmes, implemented throughout the 1950s and 1960s, provided Japanese firms with organisational capabilities with which to become world class enterprises.

Work Rules, Wages and Single Status: the Shaping of the 'Japanese Employment System' *by Shinji Sugayama*

The status hierarchy in Japanese enterprises collapsed during the tumultuous years of 'total war' and post-war democracy, and the 'Japanese employment system' was greatly affected by the 'white-collarisation of blue-collar workers'. This transformation can be seen through changes in the work rules and wages systems at Hitachi Electric from the 1930s to the 1950s. The labour ideology of the wartime planned economy, which saw enterprises as 'production communities' and assumed equality between white- and blue-collar workers, challenged the nature of employment relations. As the experience of the post-war union movement reveals, this wartime ideology exerted a pervasive influence on Japanese labour, and, during the US Occupation, it forced widespread, 'democratic' reforms on enterprise management. In consequence, the main elements of the Japanese employment system were formed and reinforced during the 1950s and 1960s.

Japanese Economic Success: Timing, Culture, and Organisational Capability

ETSUO ABE and ROBERT FITZGERALD

Meiji University and Royal Holloway, University of London

Those economic and business historians who remain unaware of the advantages of comparison must now number very few indeed, but all attempts to abandon national insularity are in practice constrained by understandable barriers of language. Because the work of Japanese scholars often remains closed, knowledge of the Japanese experience continues by necessity to be limited, despite an accelerating growth in relevant English-language works.[1] The remaining gap has significant implications, simply because Japan has become the world's second largest economy and a competitive force within international markets. Moreover, Japan's historically recent and relatively rapid success serves as an invaluable comparison for all those intrigued by the patterns and pathways of economic growth and development. Whether or not the interests of researchers and analysts lie predominantly elsewhere, Japan is an invaluable point of reference, reflecting one of the post-war world's central realities. It stands as a notable 'development model', a rich repository of case-material for those trying to unlock the secrets of economic growth; by breaking the geographical association of industrialisation with western Europe and North America, it is emulated by the newly industrialising nations of the Far East, their activities creating three globally important regions; and it is envied by those less successful countries of the post-war period, the USA and Britain.

The scale of Japan's growth is easy to demonstrate; explanation is always much more difficult. Rapid expansion after 1945 was undoubtedly assisted by the economic base which Japan had established before the Second World War, the core question being the extent of this contribution and the impact of wartime dislocation. There exists some debate over the timing of 'modern economic growth' in Japan, the definition of periods facing all the common problems of interpretation and generalisation. Some stress the importance of long-term development, trade and 'proto-industrialisation' under the Tokugawa shogunate, and Japan was commercialised before it was industrialised, but most trace modernisation from the regime's ending in 1868, the year of the

TABLE 1
JAPANESE ECONOMIC STATISTICS, 1900–1980

Year	G.D.P. Yen bn (1975=100)	Industrial Production (1980=100)	% Employed Secondary Sector (a)
1900		0.9	11.8
1910		1.2	14.9
1920		2.4	16.8
1930	14,485	3.9	17.1
1940	22,318	8.2	23.6
1950	17,275	4.2	16.6
1960	40,237	18.9	22.8
1970	118,016	66.6	28.0
1980	181,170	100.0	25.4

Note: (a) figures include all those employed in manufacturing, mining, and gas, electricity, and water utilities.

Source: *Economist, Economic Statistics, 1900–1983* (London, 1985), pp.111–20.

Meiji Restoration. After that date, Japan was assisted by the commitment of successive political factions to economic growth, and by the increasing centralisation of executive power. Fear of colonisation and nationalism were strong motivations, just as a series of wars stimulated both feelings of insecurity and levels of manufacturing output.[2] Although the government assumed an active role in economic development, entrepreneurs and business dynasties and the contribution of the Japanese firm now rightly attract the major interest of historians.[3] Kuznets locates 1874–79 as the beginnings of industrial transformation,[4] but his case is not undisputed.[5] Industry was undoubtedly the fastest growing sector of the economy between 1887–1939, expanding at an average of over six per cent per annum. Cotton textiles emerged as the country's leading manufacturing sector, although heavy industry had established a presence by the 1890s.[6] But Japan was developing from a low absolute point, and in the 1920s manufacturing output, still a minor part of the economy, was dominated by foodstuffs such as bean paste, soy sauce, and sake and by the silk and cotton textile trades. Japan had at an early date a well-developed,

TABLE 2
COMPARATIVE RATES OF GROWTH IN REAL TERMS, 1900–1983
(AVERAGE RATES PER ANNUM)

Year	Japan	U.S.A.	U.K.	W.Germany
1900-13		4.0	1.5	2.9
1920-29		3.7(b)	1.7	4.0(d)
1929-38	6.2(a)	0.1(c)	1.9	2.7
1950-60	8.8	3.3	2.7	7.8
1960-73	10.4	4.1	2.3	4.4
1973-83	3.7	2.0	2.2	1.6

Notes: (a) 1930–38; (b) 1920–28; (c) 1929–39; (d) 1925–29.

Source: *Economist, Economic Statistics, 1900–1983* (London, 1985), p.127.

urbanised market for traditional products, but the scope of industrial transformation was limited by comparison. The production of foodstuffs was conducted in relatively small-scale units, although some international enterprises, like Dai-Nihon Sugar Manufacturing, did emerge.[7] The silk industry continued to rely on traditional methods of operation, and raw silk – effectively a primary good – dominated Japan's merchandise exports. Change was more securely located in the cotton textile industry: by the 1920s, it had become internationally competitive through the use of modern technology, vertical integration, and investment in human resources, and its developing managerial hierarchies were staffed by indigenous personnel.[8] Although cotton and silk were the twin pillars of the Japanese inter-war economy, there were large and managerially complex concerns in heavy industry, chemicals, materials, and mining, many of whom were members of the *zaibatsu* conglomerates. In other words, a quarter of the largest 200 industrials in 1920, and a third in 1930, were engaged in textiles, and the biggest enterprises were shipyards supported by their own steel facilities, most notably the Kawasaki and Mitsubishi works.[9] Yet significant adjustments in Japan's overall industrial structure did occur in the inter-war years: in 1930, 35 per cent of Japan's top 200 manufacturers were to be found in machinery, primary metals, transportation equipment, and chemicals.[10] The conglomerates of Nissan and Nihon Chisso, often called the new *zaibatsu*, emerged in this period to illustrate the force of these changes. By 1940, economic growth and military requirements had established a heavy industry sector that accounted for 59 per cent of all manufacturing output; food products and textiles were responsible for 12 and 17 per cent respectively. But it is worth noting that only 7.7m of Japan's 32.5m employed labour force were engaged in manufacturing, mining, or the provision of utilities, while 14.4m worked on the land.[11] Japan seems to fit the 'Gershenkronian' model. Growth from a position of 'economic backwardness' rested on the narrow, 'uneven' development of cotton textiles and heavy industry, an example of isolated modernisation surrounded by time-locked sectors. In contemporary terms, the shipyards located at Nagasaki or Kobe were impressive in their size and organisation. The contribution of agricultural improvement in Japan to the process of rising living standards and industrialisation was not as significant as the prior case of Britain.[12] The active participation of government and the concentration of industrial activity within the *zaibatsu* also matches the requirements of Gershenkron's paradigm. For reasons of economic necessity and geo-political strategy, the 'visible hands' of government and inter-company networks supplemented the slower mechanisms of the market.[13]

The legacy left by the pre-war economy to Japan's post-war 'economic miracle' can be viewed in a number of ways. In determining the critical years, the scale of industrialisation and Japanese economic growth at various points in time are obviously useful indicators. The Japanese economy did grow by compounded rates of 6.2 per cent per annum between 1930 and 1938, but this figure is surpassed by a figure of 8.8 per cent between 1950 and 1960 and 10.4 per cent between 1960 and 1973.[14] The deleterious impact of the Second World War on Gross Domestic Product is apparent, and, as measured in constant values, it is its doubling in the 1950s and the phenomenal growth of the 1960s which is particularly remarkable. The same pattern can be seen from the index of industrial production, though even more markedly. Furthermore, Japan remained in general an overall importer of goods till the 1960s, when it finally won its worldwide reputation as an international competitor. Until 1964, more Japanese worked in agriculture, forestry and fishing than in manufacturing, the absorptive capacity of heavy industry and machinery companies being a main cause of change.[15] Like other developed countries, Japan's economy and trade balances stumbled during the oil crises of the 1970s, but, in its determination to continuously increase productivity and restrain inflation, it emerged in the mid-1980s with its relative competitiveness enhanced. Japan had, in 1990, a balance of trade worth Y6,518bn or some $52bn; by 1992, it had reached over $120bn.[16] Macro-economic indicators clearly demonstrate the Japanese 'economic miracle' to be a predominately post-war phenomenon, even if the process of transformation and industrialisation has deeper roots in the nineteenth century and, more obviously, in the 1930s and the war years. During the 1950s, Japan had to recover from the consequences of war and defeat, and the rapid expansion continued into the 1960s. The rate of economic growth sustained over such a long period and the speed of penetration into foreign markets have won the label of 'miracle', but the tag is widely recognised as a potential misnomer.[17] Japan's achievements were hard-won, and, far from being an unexpected quirk of fate, they are founded on the calculated development of economic capability.

The Japanese economy's success rests upon its strength in manufac-
turing, for the country's agriculture, distribution, services and utilities are not internationally competitive, and, sheltered by law, custom and agreement, they are relatively inefficient. As a result, Japan's productivity per head is still below that of Britain, although the difference is now marginal.[18] No country can be internationally competitive in all sectors, and it is well understood that specific industrial 'clusters' act as essential props to national advantage.[19] Any explanation of economic 'transformation' must consequently focus on specific manufacturing sectors and the development of organisational capability within industrial companies. There is, then, a further aspect to the debated legacy of the pre-war Japanese economy: to what extent had management and organisation been developed in the pre-war period, only to be extended in the post-war years? In seeking to outline and explain the transformation of Japanese manufacturing, its structure, and management, the specific historical circumstances that moulded them have to be demonstrated. As we shall see, the strategic outlook which led to the creation of organisational capabilities placed an emphasis upon co-operative alliances as well as competitive rivalry, on long-term investment and rapid growth, and on organisational adaptation and human capital, in addition to focused production, productivity, and the techniques of operations management. Japanese business objectives and organisation became in many important respects differentiated from their major competitors in the West, and any explanation of competitive advantage lies with the location of their origins. Japan's dependence on the capabilities of people and systems is a reflection of national circumstances. The country has few natural factor endowments in raw materials, energy supplies, or land, in contrast, say, to the United States or the newly industrialising Brazil; nor does it possess the geographical advantages of Hong Kong or Singapore as entrepots. A large population provides Japan with an extensive domestic market, but this current advantage is itself a result of success: it attracts interest as a 'development model' precisely because its 'transformation' occurred

from a background of low *per capita* incomes. In short, the country's factor advantages are far from *natural*; they have been *created*. Japan's manufacturing companies have had to win value-added from the raw materials they generally import, and they have done so at a level which sustains a competitive advantage over rivals with greater natural endowments. While, then, a macro-economic analysis of Japan's recent history provides necessary perspective and sweep, this approach fails in many cases to illuminate those very origins of economic success or the creation of organisational capability at an industry or company level.[20] There is no easy, single explanation which might account for the rise of Japan, just as explanations of decline in parts of North America and Europe must always be circumscribed. But the achievements of the Japanese economy do rest upon the competitive strengths of its manufacturing companies, strengths which are internal and, in the institutional relationships formed with banks, affiliated firms, and government, often external.

II

INDUSTRIAL TRANSFORMATION

By defining the period of critical change in Japanese management and organisation, it will be possible to elucidate the nature and impact of the country's industrial transformation. As one would expect, the issue is surrounded by debate, and, given the available evidence and problems of interpretation, it is dangerous to be too definitive. Some commentators have pointed to the existence of the inter-war cotton textiles industry as proof of a significant legacy in management and organisation soon to be bestowed upon the post-war Japanese economy.[21] But cotton spinning and weaving made smaller technological or organisational demands than the emerging heavy industries of engineering, shipbuilding, and steel, each production unit continuing to focus on specific process-stages. With limited examples of vertical integration, simple line management was sufficient in most textile firms, although the multifunctional form had appeared in the larger enterprises by 1940.[22] While seniority and the lifetime employment systems – perceived as two key elements of Japanese management – could be found in heavy industry after the First World War, these were generally absent in textiles, where labour management remained less systemised. The young female employees to be found in the cotton industry normally returned to their villages to marry, but heavy industry needed more committed and permanent solutions if the quantity and quality of its male labour were to be assured. Even if the heavy engineering plants of the Mitsubishi and Sumitomo *zaibatsu* had a well-organised middle management, headquarters control was weak (on definitions of *zaibatsu*, see Morikawa).[23] In order to operate effectively, many key Japanese companies before the Second World War, notably those in steel, engineering, and shipbuilding, were obliged to internalise activities within enterprises or conglomerates. These concerns became sizeable compared to many British and European counterparts, mainly because their expansion occurred from a position of 'economic backwardness'. They could not draw on a ready pool of well-trained, adaptable labour; they could not rely on market mechanisms for purchasing and marketing; capital was scarce and hard to obtain; and production systems were often rudimentary, and heavily dependent upon foreign technology and the transfer of knowledge and expertise. The attention paid, first, to the management of human resources and, second, to the flow of raw materials and finished goods shaped the objectives and structure of Japanese companies. Western corporate structures, managerial procedures, and product and production technology had to be adapted to the different circumstances and requirements, and, in necessarily giving priority to the development of human skills and resources, Japanese enterprises assumed a culture of constant personal and organisational development.[24] Success depended above all on the creation of organisational capabilities in the hiring, training and utilisation of managers and workers; on, therefore, the simplification of tasks, a clear hierarchy, and an inculcated sense of purpose and co-operation. This view of companies as a collection of people, implicit in the very word *kaisha*, is seen by many commentators as the defining element of Japanese management. Though the Japanese employment system has its roots in the period before the Second World War, it went through many stages of development and adaptation, and the same comment can be made about other aspects of management.[25]

But the self-reliance of Japanese companies, their sense of internal loyalty and vigorous competitiveness, was always combined with the establishment of networked alliances that encompassed suppliers, buyers, fellow manufacturers, and banks. Emerging manufacturers were faced with the problems of absorbing and applying new methods within a short time-span, and, by necessity, operational tasks had to be subdivided between many companies which could specialise in them.[26] This approach could have been a barrier to Japanese economic development had not the permeability of relations between companies and organisations enabled them to recoup the advantages of returns to scale. Institutional coupling was a symptom of the 'late development effect', as personal and organisational links replaced slower and inchoate market mechanisms, but it also offered particular benefits to an emerging economy. Co-operative alliances spread the risks of new investment in a country where capital was scarce, and entrepreneurial initiative and large projects were encouraged by mutual understanding between manufacturers, banks, and government. There were consequently benefits in the sharing of market and technical information, and resources could be marshalled behind a workable objective instead of being dissipated amongst rival projects. This reliance on inter-firm networks fits uneasily with Chandler's description of the large-scale, multidivisional enterprise. Japanese companies were, like the British firms he so solidly condemns, smaller than US rivals; as we have seen in the cases of Mitsubishi and Sumitomo, headquarters control was not always strong; family and personal influence, not professional top management, was characteristic of many large concerns, although ownership and control were separated in the inter-war Mitsui *zaibatsu*;[27] and manufacturing units, reliant on a nexus of contacts for line and support operations, emphasised production and productivity, and as a consequence needed only a straightforward multifunctional managerial structure.[28] It has been argued that, in accordance with Chandler's analysis, US companies were primarily driven in their mergers and reorganisation by the advantages of large-scale production systems; technological and marketing returns to scale made them focus on the flow of goods. Japanese firms had to concentrate on human resources and the adaptation of production, product and market expertise, and, in looking for 'substitutes' to incomplete market mechanisms, they evolved a different set of managerial approaches, organisational structures, and institutional relationships.[29] While Gershenkron conceived his views on 'relative backwardness' by surveying the economies of eastern and southern Europe, Japan might arguably stand as the best or clearest validator of his theories.[30]

To summarise a complicated and, to date, unresolved debate, Japan's industrialisation and the organisational capability of its companies can be traced over a long time span, beginning arguably in the nineteenth century and more certainly in the inter-war period and the war years. To accept this viewpoint, however, is not to deny the critical decades of the 1950s. As we have noted, the Japanese economy had been damaged by the Second World War, and both GDP and industrial production had fallen. Output was boosted by the USA's pursuit of the Korean War, but there was at this stage little evidence of a pending 'economic miracle'. It was over the next two decades that Japan benefited from a sustained and unprecedented rate of growth, and, in aggregate terms, the compound effects of this expansion were soon evident. This achievement was built upon developments in managerial and organisational capability. Within many companies and state agencies, crucial decisions in government–business relations, strategy, vertical and horizontal integration, managerial organisation, bank–industry linkages, labour relations, and production systems had to be made. It is the sum of these changes in internal organisation and external connections that have been endowed the title of 'Japanese management system', and they have in many particulars been given a mistakenly long pedigree, often stemming back to the nineteenth century. We must be wary, too, of generalising the Japanese experience, especially when the organisational objectives of industries and companies have undergone constant change. The majority of large enterprises, for example, are not to any substantial degree members of the *kigyo shudan*, which regrouped or formed during the 1950s, despite nominal membership (on definitions of business groupings, see Morikawa, Kikkawa and Shimotani); while many firms do have close links with banks and do carry high debt–equity ratios, Toyota has a proud history of independence and self-financing;[31] employment systems based upon lifetime employment, seniority, and fringe benefits are available only to that minority of employees working directly for corporations; while Matsushita tended to import technology, its rival Sony has always invested heavily in innovation; the Japanese have been characterised as technological imitators, as opposed to innovative adaptors, but they have responded to industrial maturity by currently spending more on research and development than their competitors.[32] Nonetheless, many of the common characteristics which compose the Japanese management system did have their birth in the 1950s, and this deepening and spreading organisational capability underwrote the 'economic miracle' of 1950–73. It was these changes which composed a means of rapid economic transformation, and, because they overcame Japan's development barriers, they are now imitated by East Asian neighbours, including mainland China.

Given the contribution of manufacturing to Japanese economic success, which factors explain the characteristics of the management systems that have underpinned the post-war competitive vigour of the *kaisha*? Clearly, a flexible, eclectic approach and analysis is required, and, in seeking this optimum, we reach an issue of enormous import in which interpretations can be delineated but never satisfactorily resolved. It is a problem that exercises many researchers of management and development studies, but it is, in fact, greatly suited to the methods and perspective of the historian. The culturally specific explanation of Japanese success seeks to identify business methods with the adaptation of deeply entrenched, traditional attitudes, namely a sense of collective spirit and commitment. Imported production methods and organisational systems are moulded by cultural norms to produce a unique management system, which cannot be wholly replicated outside Japan. The culture-free hypothesis holds Japanese management and organisational capabilities to be more deliberately established during the country's industrialisation and most obviously in the period after 1945. Technological and organisational imperatives and later international competition forced the pace of change, so shaping Japanese culture and traditional values. The choices taken and the systems founded in the 1950s have been the chief impetus behind Japan's post-war economic miracle, and, as we shall see, these were not a 'natural', cultural inheritance but a response to particular political, social and economic circumstances. An analysis of these developments and a detailed explanation of when and why they occurred is an important contribution to current debate over the nature of Japanese management, which is so often unable to separate substantive issues of strategy, systems and organisation from difficult, vaguer concepts like culture. It is to be hoped that the techniques of the business historian can unravel at least some aspects of this problem, so helping to distinguish between principal cause and effect.

III

THE CULTURALIST PERSPECTIVE

Japanese management has been perceived as essentially different to the practice of other countries, and as incapable of imitation or transfer elsewhere. If this perspective is accepted, Japanese management characteristics must stem from particular cultural traits, and the 'economic miracle' is accordingly rooted in attitudes and patterns of behaviour seemingly favourable to commercial enterprise and organisation. While culture may be relatively easy to define, the distillation of national characteristics is more difficult and open to a charge of questionable generalisation. There is, of course, no commonly accepted view of culture, but it implies those elements of human nature which are neither genetically inherited and so common to all mankind, nor those that are the province of individual personality. National cultures are attitudes and patterns of behaviour that are learned within different societies, and the results of socialisation are understood, communicated and reinforced by shared symbols, language, and expectations. In the process of 'mental programming', genetic influences, culture and individual development represent increasing degrees of human uniqueness, and, through the second level of 'programming', a society acquires those values that are associated with a significant proportion of its population. Japan was the first non-Western nation to industrialise, and the historian and management researcher's interest in cultural contrasts is to be expected. Moreover, the Japanese emphasis on companies as human organisations appeared to contradict previous assumptions about 'ideal' organisational forms. The 'Scientific Management' tradition of US companies, based on a leadership in mass production techniques and management organisation, seemingly explained their nation's post-war economic dominance, and had paid scant attention to the complexities of human motivation. Commitment would follow from the 'correct' systems and reward structures. But the association of collective and personal motivation with Japanese economic success re-opened debates about the nature of organisations. The notion of Japanese-style management acted as progenitor of the human resorces movement in the USA and Europe, where alternatives to previous methods and assumptions were sought as a means of reversing industrial failure. Attitudes at the sub-organisational level assumed the urgency once given to formal organisational and managerial structures.[33] Debates on the advent of so-called 'postmodern' organisations – replacing Fordist concepts of mass production and deskilling, and seemingly responding to new flexible technologies and segmented markets – reinforced the greater premium to be placed on the contribution of people.[34]

How, then, might we analyse and specifically define Japanese culture? It is apparent that the acquisition of cultural traits can only be explained historically, and one recurrent theme is the historical influence of geographical and physical adversity, and the concomitant need for group cohesion, collective identity, and 'uncertainty avoidance'. In order to pursue wet-paddy rice farming, the village communities of pre-industrial Japan had to be bound together, and family connections cemented this social and economic interdependence. Just as individuals were linked to families, families were linked to village communities; and village communities looked to local lords for protection and favour, just as local lords looked to the Tokugawa shogunate. Consequently, hierarchial connections had a political and military purpose as well as an economic and social one, and, within this 'vertical society', membership of a group became closely tied to personal identity. The 'vertical society' proved an enduring aspect of Japanese society and culture. In order to maintain group cohesiveness, an inculcated sense of mutual obligation, discipline, respect for elders, and seniority-based rank limited disruptive forces and the naked expression of personal ambitions. Individuals gauged their worth according to their place and respect within the collective, not by the assertion of their own views or interests. But, in addition to obligations, mutual rights and the welfare of all group members were secured through consultation procedures, and a common sense of security was preferred to direct talking and confrontation. It is further argued that the forms of Confucianism and Buddhism adopted in Japan reflected these ideals. Both encouraged propriety and respect in inter-personal relations, improvement through education, personal discipline, mutuality, a lack of ego, and group identity. It is thought by some that the mercantile houses of Mitsui, Konoike, and Sumitomo were modelled on the values and practices of village communities. The Japanese concept of *ie* or household is particular to Japan. It extends the strength of family ties to other social and economic institutions, with one signifi-cant difference. In meeting his many obligations, the head of a group is expected to appoint the personnel or successor best suited to each post, regardless of primogeniture and blood links. This outlook is the source of great organisational strength, and it facilitated at an early stage the professionalisation of management. Blood relationships are more influential within the organisations and public life of other Confucian and Buddhist societies, and large-scale enterprises in South Korea, Taiwan, and Singapore continue to be owned or managed by families. In short, Japan's traditional cultural traits were, following the Meiji Restoration of 1868, modified and transferred to its emerging industries, and it is contended that the influence on employment systems was most profound. It follows that Japan's success, like the more recent rise of other Far Eastern countries, is rooted in the adaptation of well-entrenched cultural traits or, to give it a name, the establishment of neo-Confucian societies.[35] Many writers have become jointly inter-ested in the achievements of Japan and the 'Pacific Tigers', and concluded that these countries share one common feature, namely the sense of duty, hard work and collectivism inspired by Confucianism. But there is, in fact, a very uncertain line of causation between traditional culture and successful industrialisation: the timing of developments in Japanese industrial management and the extent of their modification from village community life do make this link with pre-industrial values too frequently tenuous.

Those analysts that directly link economic success with cultural differences are supported by the work of Hofstede, which detects variations in national management systems.[36] His survey evidence rests upon 116,000 personnel questionnaires owned by IBM, and these revealed the views and attitudes of employees spread across 40 countries. He also utilised 38 other studies that, all together, looked at 39 countries. Selecting a few traits that Hofstede defines as indicative cultural attitudes, he looks for those differences in values that require organisational responses. So, the Japanese emphasis on 'uncertainty avoidance' and social stability may require guarantees of job security, while Anglo-American economies are based on labour market mobility; individualism encourages personal incentives, but collectivism remunerates group achievement and minimises pay differentials. In concluding that organisations are 'culture-bound', Hofstede believes that there are no universal answers to the problems of organisation and management.[37] Any definition of 'Japanese management' should be circumscribed by caveats, precisely because perceptions have been shaped only by the practice of large-scale manufacturing companies, and little difference is generally allowed even within this narrow group. Nevertheless, there are a number of characteristics regarded as commonplace to the Japanese corporation. These include the identification of employees with firms, a collective spirit, and a sense of duty and mutual obligation (*on* and *giri*). Internal labour markets are supported by lifetime employment, seniority-based pay and promotion, twice-yearly bonuses, and welfare benefits, and companies are willing to spend resources on training schemes for workers and managers. Quality circles, production-line flexibility, and a mission for continuous improvement (*kaizen*) are linked with Just-in-Time systems and capital investment, and formal hierarchies are combined with informal consultation procedures. High debt–equity ratios and close bank–industry relations are preferred to shareholder control, and, despite highly competitive domestic and international markets, companies co-operate on mutually beneficial projects, sometimes with the support of trade associations and government agencies. The cohesiveness of Japanese firms can be attributed to the national characteristic of collectivism and the vertical society, the product of particular historical circumstances. Loyalty to a firm is balanced by guarantees of security and advancement, and disruption is avoided by the culturally understandable consultation procedures that supplement 'correct' relations within the hierarchy. While Western employees see their employment in terms of function – clerk, engineer, or factory operative – the Japanese view themselves as members of a specific firm. Quality circles successfully operate in Japan because there is little need for supervisory control, and Just-in-Time systems gain from a dislike of waste and inefficiency precisely because they are mutually damaging to company and individual. Confucian attitudes towards personal improvement, education, and savings are reflected in investment levels, training schemes, savings ratios, and the sacrifice of immediate consumption. The corporate power of managers relative to shareholders increases the employees' sense of owning their company, and the national cohesiveness of the Japanese is expressed through strong links with other companies and the government.

IV

ECONOMICS AND SOCIOLOGY

The culturally specific view of management and organisational forms –
themselves the very origins of competitive advantage and economic
success – has been refined by authors following the work of Granovetter.[38]
He rejects the dichotomy between cultural and organisational factors
as an example of unnecessary reductionism. It leads, in one case, to
an 'over-socialised' view, where economic growth is explained only
through the influence of transforming cultures. Just as Max Weber fused
Protestantism with European and North American capitalism, the
characteristics of Far Eastern businesses are symbiotically joined to
neo-Confucianism.[39] The 'under-socialised' view, the other case, depicts
management and organisation as shaped by universally applicable
economic factors, transaction costs and technological imperatives,
and culture's influence is viewed as peripheral and transitory. Those
who perceive the post-war internationalisation of the world economy as a
prelude to its globalisation or homogenisation are naturally drawn to a
culturally free perspective. By offering a range of cross-national contingent factors which explain the rationale of various organisational forms,
Chandler and Mintzberg clearly fall into the second tradition.[40] Granovetter states that organisations are formed in response to both social
and economic factors; they are 'achieved' over time, and they have a
unique combination of characteristics because of their own objectives and
the particular context within which they operate. For each given situation,
there are degrees of 'relative autonomy' and 'relative dependence'
between economic and social realities, and organisational forms are
the result of many compromises which may optimise opportunities.
Granovetter sums up his view with the term 'embeddedness', and by
this he means that different societies require different organisational
solutions, and that organisations become 'embedded' within their specific
contexts. Neo-Confucianism represents a fusion of both cultural and
economic considerations. Far Eastern companies have encouraged
economically efficient but also socially cohesive beliefs and values, just
as organisational practices that on the surface appear 'economically
rational' have been adapted whenever they are revealed as counter-
productive, socially divisive, and, by definition, inefficient. Although he
adopts an analytically different approach, Etzioni reaches similar conclusions on this issue. Concentrating on the subject of human motivatation
within organisations, he argues that people work for 'love', 'fear' or
money, and that the nature of relationships will be determined by
which factor is the more dominant. 'Love' suggests mutual identity and

co-operation, so relations will be 'normative'; in the other two cases, they are 'coercive' and 'remunerative'. Though feelings of coercion and alien-ation can always prove disruptive, advanced nations and organisations tend to be a combination of remunerative-calculative and normative-moral associations; they are, in other words, a mixture of individualistic or collectivist motivations.[41] Far Eastern businesses, it would follow, work through shared values, agreement and compliance, and require less coercion and fewer monetary incentives than Western counterparts. But there are no absolutes: every organisation is 'achieved' and combines all three aspects of human motivation, and each solution will be deter-mined by specific differences in the 'relative autonomy' and 'relative dependence' of both cultural and economic factors.

In short, researchers have been offered coherent reasons for avoiding narrow interpretations; they are thereby urged to understand and explain the interwoven economic, political, social and cultural dimensions of human agency. These lessons are, of course, well known and appreciated, if on occasions overlooked. How might this eclecticism elucidate the means by which actual organisations are created and developed, and how do we link the varied elements of organisation with determinant organisational capability and economic success? This is not a question which can be answered abstractly, because competitiveness is itself a relative concept and organisational capabilities are formed in response to particular historical and environmental circumstances. In any specific example it is not inherently true that both economic and cultural factors have proved equally important. So Granovetter's concept of 'relative autonomy' and 'relative dependence', the extent to which economics or national culture have to be accommodated, merely asks rather than answers the question of how a firm's organisational capability may become 'embedded'. The analyst still has to weigh the impact of each factor or agent of change, even if they are subsequently 'fused' into a single social and economic reality. In pursuit of answers, the difficulties that arise from the exploration of cause and effect remain. The historian – naturally exercised by the perspective of time – must additionally separate short-term factors from those which have an enduring impact. In explaining the roots of Japanese success, we have seen how the 'economic miracle' was shaped by both the pre-war and post-war growth of industry. In which case, the social and cultural accommodations made during a process of industrial transfor-mation may in the long term be undermined if they do not serve an economic purpose, especially if domestic and international markets are competitive; they may in consequence be phenomena best explained and understood through the language of economics.

National cultures do undergo change, and some writers too easily equate the beliefs and values of the Tokugawan shogunate with modern-day Japan. Notions of neo-Confucianism are more acceptable because they assume cultural adaptation as a response to economic, political and social considerations. The issue centres upon the extent of the adaptation: culture when compared to the demands of economics may appear infinitely mutable; on the other hand, cultural norms can demonstrate an ability to endure, despite the needs of 'economic rationality'. Granovetter's approach has undoubted benefits: it challenges what may in many cases be a false dichotomy between economic and cultural explanations of organisational capability. The historian has to recognise the practical interdependence of these factors, but, in tracing their effect and weighing their significance, clarity frequently demands their separation. The same cultural attributes that are now used to explain Japanese industrial prowess were once used to explain their backwardness.[42] While it may be true that Japanese society encourages stability, Hofstede's concept of 'uncertainty avoidance' overlooks the way in which large Far Eastern corporations mix employee security with constant change in manufacturing techniques and products. The sharing of risk through co-operative alliances similarly enhances 'bold' strategies of entrepreneurial initiative and the Japanese *kaisha*'s preference for rapid growth. Japan's industrial transformation reveals a willingness to adapt, not an reaction to traditionalism, and this ability to change depended on the creation of new economic institutions and companies. Arguably, groupism inhibits innovation and decision-making, and Confucianism is often associated with a suspicion of physical labour. Neither of these notions would assist industrial endeavour. Wiener's belief in the undermining of British competitiveness by the cultural attitudes that emerged in the late Victorian period can be criticised on many points, not least because many elements of current British culture when compared to aspects of Confucianism are conducive to business.[43] By seeking the roots of industrial organisations and economic success in differing national cultures, we are frequently offered a blanket explanation that is too easy, too assumptive, often 'lazy'. The process of Japanese industrialisation and the development of its competitive organisational capabilities can be explained more definitively.

V

INSTITUTIONS AND ORGANISATIONAL CAPABILITY

Major differences between national examples of capitalism and their comparative success have frequently been traced to the timing and pathways of industrialisation. Britain achieved industrial pre-eminence in a number of industries that were characterised by focused production units and domestic and international networks which often linked individuated process-stages. As Chandler has stated in *Scale and Scope*, US business at the turn of the century was increasingly able to exploit the linked advantages of mass production and technological progress, those aspects of the so-called 'second industrial revolution'. Rising demand at home, its relative homogeneity, and specific factors such as transportation and distribution needs in the USA additionally encouraged the founding of large-scale, managerial enterprises with organisational capabilities that in turn proved domestically and internationally competitive. Arising disparities in productivity and living standards between the two countries are duly located in the size, governance and organisation of their leading manufacturing companies.[44] There is dispute over the causes and implications of Anglo-American contrasts, Chandler indicating a failure of British management, Hannah, most notably, pointing to differences in market demand and structure and to consequent problems of interpretation.[45] While Chandler is convinced of the similarities to be discovered in the historical experiences of the USA and Germany, other polemicists have vigorously highlighted the gulf between Anglo-American and European versions of capitalism.[46] It is said that both the US and British economies have shown a predominant reliance on competitive mechanisms, although, it should be added, restrictive practices continued to be influential in Britain until after the Second World War. Potentially, it is the nature of institutional links and their ability to foster competitiveness, change, and investment, their purpose, context, and influence at a given stage of economic development which is critical, collusion in Britain being negative and costly rather than a means of optimising and enhancing value-added along a production chain of varied participants. The institutional links of restrictive practices, even if one accepts their overall efficacy, were minimalist, hindering rationalisation, or, alternatively, forestalling the integrated co-ordination of strategic and operational interests. As a consequence, a lack of co-operative arrangements and interlocking shareholding between Anglo-American companies was and is reflected in the relations between government and business; a reliance on equity financing has deflected attention from a subtle range of bank–industry contacts; and shareholder influence and accounting systems have promoted short-term profits at the expense of long-term growth and investment in production facilities, research, and human resources. Fruin's *The Japanese Enterprise System* is frequently seen as a counterpart to *Scale and Scope*, and, in it, the mixture of co-operative structures and intense competition in Japan is contrasted with the USA. Although there are obvious differences, and important ones in some cases, there are too evident parallels between Japan and Europe in mutual shareholding, bank–industry arrangements, the nature of corporate governance, and long-term strategic horizons, just as there are affinities between capitalism in the United States and Britain. Fruin's book amounts to a major monograph that is comprehensive and full of new data, especially on the comparative size of Japanese manufacturers, but his conclusions have been widely established for some time.[47] Although he continuously pays homage to Chandler, and rightly so, his work intentionally or not is critical of the idea that national economic success in the twentieth century has been linked to the type of managerial enterprise so commonly associated with the multidivisional form and the United States. Given variations in economic structure and the changing fortunes of Britain, the USA, Germany, and Japan, it is problematic to deploy one form of organisation as a panacea, and economic and industrial structures should be evaluated by the extent to which they enable in any given case the optimal combination of market mechanisms, technology and company organisation. Historical and economic circumstances determined variations in pathways to industrialisation or enhanced competitiveness, and the successful adoption of systems and the degree to which they met and then continued to meet specific developmental requirements will help to elucidate national variations in the rates of post-war growth. The market and institutional structures and the production strategies which evolved in Japan were effective responses to the demands of its industrialisation, and, as a result of enhancement and adaptation, it produced an industrial system with the capacity to generate a range of competitive advantages. It is possible to say that those co-operative alliances which are distinctive to Japanese economic institutions are rooted in a Confucian culture and a greater sense of collective identity, but this ignores the complexity and rationale behind Japan's emergence as an economic superpower. A set of given values may have assisted or facilitated the choice of pathway, but it weighs light against the plausibility of alternative perspectives.

What might explain the perceived characteristics of the Japanese industrial system? Industrialisation was encouraged by a government that was anxious to overcome its military, diplomatic and economic vulnerability, and domestic conditions and relationships with East Asia also favoured the process of development. At the time of the Meiji Restoration, Japan already had a number of labour-intensive workshop industries, and a distribution system for both food and merchandise that supplied a large, urbanised market. The country possessed trading links with neighbouring nations, and the cotton industry, growing out of the traditional silk business, soon had a number of ready export markets, eventually displacing rivals from the Indian sub-continent and elsewhere. A combination of political and economic factors, then, favoured rapid industrialisation, yet success was dependent on the finding of substitutes for absent markets in supply, distribution, capital, and labour, and on access to imported technology and skills. The Japanese state and business were committed to the creation of indigenous enterprise, co-operating through joint ventures for as long as was necessary, and the size and nature of the Japanese market was to prove advantageous enough to act as a testing-ground for international competitiveness. It is common-place that the 'late development effect' conditioned the evolution of the Japanese industrial system, and that an iterative historical experience forced participants to learn different lessons to those consequent upon the more drawn out, market-orientated industrialisation of Britain and the USA. During the 1870s, the state had a direct role in the creation of infrastructure, including the telegraph and the railways, but, in addition to the construction of armaments factories and shipyards which were needed for government purposes, it attempted at first to be a widescale substitute agency for the market. The Ministry of Industry, for example, was charged with the creation of a single, unified telegraph system, but, in order to obtain and service its equipment, it also sponsored and then took over its suppliers, the Tanaka Works. After 1885, the government abandoned a policy of centrally directed industrialisation, and began to divest itself of many facilities, important assets subsequently passing to private concerns.[48] The *zaibatsu* conglomerates which emerged during this period – the largest four being Mitsui, Mitsubishi, Yasuda, and Sumitomo – were vital to Japanese industrialisation in heavy industry and chemicals, and they were key purchasers of government plants. Privatisation had the fortuitous effect of creating companies or plant of a comparatively large scale, and these had the size and resources to under-take a range of related activities, their activism and contacts facilitating new ventures. In some cases, notably Mitsui, they used banking and trading connections to further their newly acquired industrial interests, and the prices paid to the government were low enough not to choke off future investment. Mitsubishi bought the Nagasaki shipyard in 1884, and, in 1893, Mitsui bought the Tanaka Works, the very operation which became the forerunner of Toshiba. Nonetheless, the state's continued commitment to the development of infrastructure can be seen by its incor-poration of several companies into the Japanese National Railway in 1907. It also assisted in the importation of technology, and controlled inward trade and investment.[49] It is apparent, not least from this volume, that state intervention increased from the early 1930s onwards. The sheltering of Japanese industry, including an emerging motor vehicle industry, became more pronounced, and tariff barriers, quotas and ownership regulations prevented the building of organisational capability being undermined by overwhelming foreign competition. During the years of armed conflict, many of the government's reforms in production organisation and human resources permanently shaped Japanese industrial management. In a subsequent period, the Ministry of Industry and Trade controlled a range of economic levers with which to influence and coordinate investment decisions. Johnson, in his well known study of Japanese-style corporatism, points to a substantial degree of continuity during the peace-time policy making of the 1950s, although there was an increasing incidence of 'administrative guidance' in place of the statutory order.[50] MITI conspicuously curtailed the rivalry of Sumitomo Steel and Kawasaki Steel, and used business contacts and co-operative mechanisms to concentrate resources on strategic investments, the aim being to reduce risks and maximise returns to scale. In the 1950s, the Japanese steel industry required modernising; the government's policy of enhanced industrialisation and economic growth was intricately linked with a modern steel industry; and the particular economics of steel-making necessitated large-scale, capital-intensive plant.[51] Yet the Ministry's impact outside heavy industry and on the new consumer enterprises of cars and electronics was by no means as significant, the forces of vigorous competition shaping their strategies and alliance networks.[52]

While, as a result, it would be right to emphasise the useful role government has played in the development of a 'backward' economy, it would be wrong not to stress the primary importance of private industry. In his comprehensive analysis of the *zaibatsu*, Hidemasa Morikawa stresses the way in which these family-owned holding companies could initiate a series of unrelated developments. They could provide the financial, supply, and marketing contacts which were essential to the development of enterprises engaged in steel, shipbuilding and chemicals, when market contacts and infrastructure were still emergent. Large firms, assisted by a network of alliances, had to take the initiative. At the heart of several *zaibatsu* was a main bank, and linked general trading companies, the *sogoshosha*, offered access to raw materials, overseas market entry, and distributive returns to scale.[53] Mitsui's origins were those of bankers and merchants, but by 1936 it had 101 affiliated companies operating in mining, metals manufacture, machinery, textiles, and food. There were, naturally, variations in the origins of famous companies, but associative enterprise was a common pattern. Hitachi, for one, began as the electrical machinery repair shop of Kuhara Mining, which later became Nippon Sangyo and the owner of Nissan Chemical

Industries and Nissan Motors.[54] As Gershenkron states, the transformation of backward economies has rested on the development of leading companies concentrated in a narrow range of sectors, advanced production units existing alongside untransformed industrial or agricultural interests. As in the case of state 'guidance', effective inter-company contacts enabled scarce resources in capital, management, and technology to be concentrated on essential projects, and acted as an essential mechanism of risk reduction for new, large enterprises hindered by their dearth of experience and organisational capability. Both government and large businesses had to appreciate that a developing economy could support a more limited number of rival enterprises, and both returns to scale and returns on the initial investment were dependent on co-operation and information flows through state agencies and business networks. On the other hand, as new entrants often supplying an 'undeveloped' market, Japanese companies were still unable to achieve the scale efficiencies of overseas rivals, and institutional connections between banks, producers, suppliers, and distributors were able to reduce transactions costs in a way that procured compensating economies of scope. Permeability and institutional co-ordination helps explain differences in the size of companies and the depths of corporate managerial hierarchy between Japan and the United States and other Western countries. By the inter-war period, it can be said that *zaibatsu* companies were strategically interrelated but operationally separate.[55]

The *zaibatsu* were formally disbanded after the Second World War,[56] but the economic logic of co-operative alliances encouraged the same groups to re-coalesce as *kigyo shudan*. Mutual shareholdings created a network of allies, so replacing the *zaibatsu* structure of parent company and subsidiaries, and company groups continued to facilitate investment and the flow of personnel and know-how in a critical period of reconstruction and further economic development.[57] In this volume, Morikawa expands on his analysis of the *zaibatsu*, arguing that the managerial changes which occurred during the 1950s in Japan's largest companies strengthened an industrial system of beneficial co-operative alliances. The new chief executives were either internal, salaried appointees or entrepreneurial owners, and both of these groups had a deep understanding of their concerns and their employees' confidence and support. Their ability to attract the co-operation of banks, business allies and government facilitated the rapid industrialisation of post-war Japan. The Japanese tradition of the most able candidate and not the family heir being appointed to the head of a group or organisation – the survival of the group being paramount – has assisted the process of managerial professionalisation.[58] The ways in which a horizontal network of alliances bolstered managerial independence – indeed assisted the very emergence of managerial enterprise – is also discussed by Kikkawa. Mutual share-holding was an alternative to interference from outside owners, and it removed the insecurity which followed the *ziabatsu* dissolution and other measures, so enabling firms to plan for long-term growth rather than short-term profits. Joint projects within the *kigyo shudan* groups or between large companies continued to be favoured during a time when large-scale investments remained risky. In other words, alliances had economic and strategic utility, and, as the Japanese economy developed and as companies grew in organisational capability, individual firms secured greater independence of action. Six major coalitions emerged: three were based on the old, typical *zaibatsu* of Mitsubishi, Mitsui, and Sumitomo, and the remaining three of Daiichi Kangin, Fuji and Sanwa were formed around city banks.[59] The *kigyo shudan*, established to guar-antee shareholder stability and managerial control, became a valuable vehicle of rapid, co-ordinated industrialisation, but their usefulness to a maturing economy was not so apparent. The very same point can be made about the role of the government and the Ministry of International Trade and Industry. Whatever the contribution made by a cultural inclination to collective action, it does little to explain the rationale behind business alliances or state intervention, and fits uneasily with post-war changes in their objectives, most notably the growing independence of individual companies. The petrochemicals industry was created in the 1950s and 1960s through group investment, but, as the individual companies devel-oped their own capabilities and market knowledge, they rather than their alliances became the primary actors.

Shimotani concentrates on the founding of distribution networks by Japanese corporations, and these and the implementation of other vertical connections within *kigyo keiretsu* were also responses to the needs of a rapidly industrialising economy. They partnered financial and production links in the management of the value chain, and Matsushita, like Mitsubishi Electric,[60] founded its distribution network in the 1920s. Many enterprise groups which prospered in the post-war period – companies like Matsushita, Sony, Fujitsu, Honda, Toyota, Kao and Canon – depended more on binding vertical linkages and were not coalition members. Moreover, during the 1950s, it was investment in essential marketing channels that enabled the full development of both the electronics and the automobile industries. Tatsuki explores the long history and structure of Japanese retailing, illustrating why it was un-suited to the new consumer industries of the 1950s. Traditional methods continued alongside innovations, and economic growth from a position of relative backwardness sustained the duality that is symptomatic of

Japanese retailing. The vertical links between manufacturing and finance are the subject of Okazaki's article. The support offered by city banks as the main banks of many industrial concerns was boosted by a network of intricate, complementary institutional arrangements and the state's regulatory framework. In the 1950s, both the Ministry of Finance and the Ministry of International Trade and Industry maintained the liquidity of banks and manufacturing, and directed scarce capital resources to projects deemed essential to rapid economic expansion. By substituting resort to the stock market, institutional alliances and governmental regulation shaped a system of debt financing, and through mutual share-holding helped secure the managerial control which underpinned business strategies of long-term growth. As we shall see, the instruments of 'Japanese management' were predicated on the subsequent freedom and ability of companies to invest in research and development, technology, production facilities, and human resources. There was limited opportunity for mass production in Japan until the 1950s, and manufacturing was conducted on a comparatively small scale. Managerial pressures on the *zaibatsu* did increase in the inter-war period, but organisational structures were not like those of Chandler's modern corporation. As Morikawa argues, it was the rapid growth of the 1950s and the concomitant expansion of individual companics and their operations that finally necessitated the completion of Japan's 'managerial revolution'. The relatively small size of operational units – whether or not they were members of groups – can be attributed to the problems of developing organisational capability at a fast speed and from a position of 'backwardness'. The adoption of new technologies, the recruitment and training of personnel, and the efficient organisation of production lines were more easily and more effectively achieved in factories that focused on a single or dominant product. Moreover, inchoate markets and low per capita incomes did not support the strategies of mass production then being implemented by giant US corporations. Economies of scope and 'permeability' between companies bestowed countervailing advantages to those losses in scale that were consequent upon the timing of Japan's industrialisation. Important developments did occur in the post-war period. In the strategic steel industry, cost reduction was perceived as a critical success factor, and coastal plants employing the latest technology supplied both indigenous and export demand. The reputation of the *kaisha* as 'learning organisations' can be attributed to their initial need to imitate and improve on the practices of overseas firms,[61] and this specific dimension of corporate culture, captured in the byword of *kaizen*, stretches from constant product innovation to an emphasis on the training and adaptability of employees, but it is most notable in attitudes towards production management. The Japanese industrial system is the result of a unique combination of government, business alliances, individual companies and markets, which naturally shows both the legacy of its beginnings and subsequent adjustments. The role of MITI, *kigyo shudan*, and *keiretsu* have attracted particular notice, and, historically, they have supplied critical capabilities that would not otherwise have evolved. But they are supportive of the activities and competitive advantages that reside within individual companies, and the *kaisha* have particular traditions and strengths in production and human resource management. In comparing Japanese with British firms, Koya and McMillan detected a clear Japanese bias for the production and personnel function over the concern of the British for accounting and finance.[62] When Akio Morita, the chairman of Sony, made his often-repeated remark about British industry having too many accountants and too few engineers, he was well supported in his views.

It is factory-level organisation which has been the driving force behind Japanese competitiveness. In this volume, Udagawa outlines the well-known cases of vehicle manufacturers Toyota and Nissan, indicating how technology acquisition, scarce resources and the nature of indigenous market demand stimulated 'lean production' methods and quality control programmes.[63] During the 1950s and 1960s, Japanese companies developed methods and systems which proved more efficient and productive than the mass manufacturing approaches of world leaders in the USA and Europe. A shortage of capital discouraged the long production runs of US manufacturers, in any case inappropriate to the Japanese market, and the need for training ruled out 'British-style' reliance on individual work skills and piece rates. A system originally conceived as a means of minimising inventory and land usage soon offered the economy and quality advantages of flexible manufacturing. An emphasis on engineering and operations stemmed directly from an industrial structure of focused factories and a strategic awareness of the need to overcome 'economic backwardness'. Furthermore, the logic of 'learning organisations' being focused in their activities and opting for vertical integration encouraged that special feature of Japanese manufacturing success, effective management of the supply chain. Sugayama discusses, in turn, changes instituted by firms in the management of employment relationships. He concentrates on the 'white collarisation' of blue-collar workers, and on the development of factory communities which could inspire the sort of loyalty and motivation required of a war economy and then peacetime reconstruction. Those well-known attributes of human organisation within Japanese corporations – mutual respect, consultation, seniority, single status, lifetime employment, and eventually company unionism –

formed the components or results of this shift in business policy. As in the case of Gordon's comprehensive study of Japanese heavy industry,[64] Sugayama's analysis of electrical companies deals with the period between 1920 and 1960, and it is not a story of culturally determined, ingrained consensus. Stable employment conditions in exchange for corporate loyalty were not a commonplace inheritance of the Tokugawan household society, and were gradually implemented only in a number of large-scale companies.[65] A series of conflicts, in some cases bitter and class inspired, had to be resolved and systems had to be continuously modified in line with organisational and economic imperatives before what is known as the Japanese employment system emerged. During the period of Japan's rapid industrialisation, manufacturers had to use employees frequently unacquainted with factory labour, and, from the 1920s onwards, companies paid increasing attention to the employment function. A ready supply of employees and skills not being available, the traditional labour market had to be supplemented by the internalisation of activities and the active creation of organisational capabilities. The difficulties of hiring, moulding and then retaining a workforce during the critical years of industrial transformation bestowed on Japanese companies their particular traditions of human resource management. As Morikawa has stated, this awareness of personnel questions can be seen in the growing procurement of graduates and in the establishment of deep managerial cadres, particularly in the post-war years. Between 1920 and 1960, new practices began to replace less permanent, more alienating forms of employment, which had operated despite the Japanese inclination for group identity and notions of the vertical society. If the cultural values of the group proved useful to the organisation of rising corporations, they had to be imposed on an industrial system where they had become absent.[66] Life-time employment, seniority, company-based training, bonuses, single status, welfare schemes, company unions, and consultative decision-making fulfilled the economic and organisational requirements of corporations, and by the 1960s benefited those 30 per cent of the Japanese workforce permanently employed by large companies. The reasons behind the famed 'dual economy' complemented an emphasis on production organisation, and the expenses of an internal labour market were partly afforded by the structure of focused factories and extensive contracting out to suppliers, where employment conditions were not comparable. As we have seen, these evolving institutional arrangements suited a manufacturing sector with limited possibilities for return to scale, which, nevertheless, had competitively advantageous repercussions on the management of the value chain. It is worth recognising how subcontracting became more pervasive during the Second

World War, as large firms attempted to keep pace with military orders, and that it was more fully developed after 1945.[67] Large enterprises like Toyota and Matsushita Electrical Industries have created production and distribution networks that utilise hundreds of firms, although, it should be noted, others like Kao and Canon have preferred to internalise operations. A permanent, highly motivated, but flexible workforce enabled Japanese corporations to maximise their investments in production technology, whilst facilitating in the post-war period a growing attention to quality control. Identification with the company, that sense of the business belonging to its employees, has undoubtedly been boosted by circumstances of managerial control, low owner influence, and long-term planning horizons.

The strengths of the Japanese corporation were widely investigated and revealed in 1985 through Abegglen and Stalk's famous book, *Kaisha*. These companies were portrayed as committed competitors, and their strategies were rooted in a bias for growth. With the domestic economy expanding rapidly, any other approach gave rivals future revenues, market knowledge, and other advantages which soon became insuperable. Nor did this preference for sales over dividends concern Japanese shareholders: in time, capital gains brought returns which were superior to those obtainable in the West. A so-called conservative, traditional society possessed companies which had the resources and the contacts to initiate new product lines in a single-minded manner, a policy that helped to maintain fast growth strategies. First mover advantages have as a consequence been less pronounced in Japan, where exit rates amongst the list of the highest 200 manufacturers have been comparatively higher than in other advanced nations.[68] Needless to say, government agency, co-operative alliances, and bank–industry relationships – all stemming from the specific historical development of Japanese business – assisted in the *kaisha*'s successful strategies and operations. In difficult times, Japanese companies had institutional relationships which allowed them to invest more in production techniques, research and development, and human resources. Foremost enterprises were able to exploit their strengths in production methods and human resources, first through low-cost manufacturing, but latterly in the 1980s through a growing incidence of product differentiation.[69] An ability to imitate and improve products and production processes has similarly been transformed into a technological lead. As a percentage of sales, expenditures by the *kaisha* have in many cases overtaken those of major foreign competitors, just as the total amount spent on non-defence research and development in Japan, as a ratio of GDP, had surpassed Western countries.[70] The essential components of Japan's industrial power, their characteristics influenced by the period and nature of its economic growth, have been developed since the nineteenth century; the origins of the Japanese industrial system can be more clearly seen in changes which occurred after 1920; and the two decades or so which followed the ending of the Second World War witnessed the completion and improvement of that system, unprecedented economic growth, and the achievement of international competitiveness. The capabilities of Japanese manufacturing – resulting from the complex interaction of factory-level organisation, markets, business networks, and governments – were naturally unique, but the forces of competitiveness were well understood by the *kaisha*, just as they were appreciated by government. Increasing economic internationalisation has reinforced these lessons. However much the distinctiveness of this system was assisted by tradition, especially in the management of human resources, the economic and organisational rationale can be explained in historical terms which override responses of cultural incomprehensibility. Japan had evolved an economy with government–network–business boundaries which optimised the chances offered by the timing and circumstances of its industrialisation. The ability of its manufacturing companies to weather the oil crises and world depressions of the 1970s – indeed, their ability to improve competitive advantage – revealed the effectiveness of that system. The 'mature' economy which had been firmly established by 1980 had brought product differentiation, technological leadership, and companies which in several cases rival their US counterparts in size. The individual *kaisha* has reduced its need of government assistance or guidance, and is potentially less concerned by the effective ties of business networks. Debt financing, formerly facilitated by strategies of maximum sales, is in a period of slower economic growth being counterbalanced by shareholding. In meeting emerging and effective rivals in neighbouring East Asia, Japan is undergoing eventful shifts in industrial structure, and its corporations are increasingly investing overseas, gaining supply-side advantages in developing countries, and securing markets in the West. Domestic difficulties and a global fall in demand during the early 1990s have undermined profitability, and threatened for the first time that very symbol of post-war advance, the guarantee of lifetime employment. It is too early to decide whether a system that was created within a 'backward' economy will be equally successful in the years of its 'maturity', and it seems unlikely, but the strategic and operational decisions that were taken in the post-war decades have convincingly secured the permanence of Japanese industrial power.

NOTES

1. It is customary to acknowledge the great value which English speakers place on Proceedings of the Fuji International Business History Conference, published since 1976, and the *Japanese Business History Yearbook*. But neither is a replacement, even with the backing of numerous English monographs and articles, for the greater weight of inaccessible works. One statistic will have to serve as some measure of the depth of research carried out in Japanese: while Britain's Association of Business Historians has nearly 200 members, the Business History Association of Japan can boast about 800. While economic history in Japan became associated in the post-war years with Marxist intellectuals, business history attracted those of other traditions, especially those employed in faculties of commerce and management.
2. The succession of wars includes: the Sino-Japanese of 1894–95, the Russo-Japanese War of 1904–5, the First World War, conflict in Manchuria and China in the 1930s and 1940s, and, lastly, the Second World War.
3. This emphasis is apparent in J. Hirschmeier, *The Origins of Entrepreneurship in Meiji Japan* (Cambridge, 1964), and is noted in H. Rosovsky and K. Yamamura, 'Entrepreneurial Studies in Japan: An Introduction', *Business History Review*, Vol.XLIV (1970), pp.4–6.
4. S. Kuznets, *The Economic Growth of Nations: Total Output and Production Structure* (Harvard, 1971), p.24. See also idem, *Modern Economic Growth Rate, Structure and Spread* (Yale, 1966), especially for its detailed definition of 'modern economic growth'.
5. H. Rosovsky (ed.), *Industrialisation in Two Systems* (New York, 1966), p.92; W.W. Rostow, *The Stages of Economic Growth* (Cambridge, 1971), p.38.
6. K. Ohkawa and M. Shinohara (eds.), *Patterns of Japanese Economic Development: A Quantitative Appraisal* (Yale, 1979), p.135; R. Clark, *The Japanese Company* (Yale, 1979), pp.1–43; J. Hirschmeier and T. Yui, *The Development of Japanese Business, 1600–1973* (London, 1975), pp.200–12.
7. Y. Suzuki, *Japanese Management Structures, 1920–1980* (London, 1991), pp.24–6; M. Fruin, *The Japanese Enterprise System: Competitive Strategies and Cooperative Structures* (Oxford, 1992), pp.329–35.
8. W. Mass and W. Lazonick, 'The British Cotton Industry and International Competitive Advantage: The State of the Debates', *Business History*, Vol.32 (1990), pp.9–65; G. Clark, 'Why Isn't the Whole World Developed: Lessons from the Cotton Mills', *Journal of Economic History*, Vol.XLVII (1987); S. Yonekawa, 'University Graduates in Japanese Enterprises before the Second World War', *Business History*, Vol.26 (1984); idem, 'The Growth of Cotton Spinning Firms: A Comparative Study', in A. Okochi and S. Yonekawa (eds.), *The Textile Industry and its Business Climate* (Tokyo, 1982); H. Morikawa, 'The Increasing Power of Salaried Managers in Japan's Large Corporations', in W.D. Wray (ed.), *Managing Industrial Enterprise: Cases from Japan's Prewar Experience* (Cambridge, MA, 1989); Y. Suzuki, *Japanese Management Structures*, pp.13–43.
9. Fruin, *Japanese Enterprise System*, pp.116, 164, 329–50.
10. Ibid., p.167. See also H. Morikawa, *Zaibatsu: The Rise and Fall of Family Enterprise Groups in Japan* (Tokyo, 1992); and Suzuki, *Japanese Management Structures*, pp.44–74.
11. *Economist, Economic Statistics, 1900–1983* (London, 1985), p.118.
12. See Y. Hayami, *A Century of Agricultural Growth in Japan* (Tokyo, 1975); M. Nakamura, *Kindai Nippon Jinushisei Shi Kenkyu* (*Studies in the Landlord–Tenant System in Modern Japan*) (Tokyo, 1979); H. Niwa, *Jinushisei no Keisei to Kozo* (*The Formation of the Landlord–Tenant System and its Structure*) (Tokyo, 1982); H. Ohashi, *Chiho Sangyo Kakumei no Kenkyu* (*Local Studies in the Industrial Revolution of Japan*) (Tokyo, 1975); Y. Sakai, *Nippon Jinushisei Shi Kenkyu Josetu* (*Studies in the Landlord–Tenant System of Japan*) (Tokyo, 1978).
13. I. Inkster, 'Meiji Economic Development in Perspective: Revisionist Comments upon

the Industrial Revolution in Japan', *Journal of Economic History*, Vol.37 (1977); idem, *Japan as a Development Model: Relative Backwardness and Technological Transfer* (Bochum, 1980); S. Ishikawa, *Economic Development in Asian Perspective* (Tokyo, 1967); idem, *Essays on Technology, Employment, and Institutions in Economic Development* (Tokyo, 1981); W.W. Lockwood, *The State and Economic Enterprise in Japan* (Princeton, NJ, 1965). See A. Gershenkron, *Economic Backwardness in Historical Perspective* (Cambridge, MA 1962).

14. *Economist, Economic Statistics*, p.127.
15. Ibid., p.118; T. Nakamura, *The Postwar Japanese Economy: its Development and Structure* (Tokyo, 1981), p.155.
16. *Facts and Figures of Japan* (Tokyo, 1991), p.47.
17. World Bank, *The East Asian Miracle: Economic Growth and Public Policy* (Oxford, 1993), pp.1–8.
18. See, for example, W. Eltis, D. Fraser and M. Ricketts, 'The Lessons for Britain from the Superior Economic Performance of Germany and Japan', *National Westminister Bank Quarterly Review* (1992), pp.2–22.
19. See M. Porter, *The Competitive Advantage of Nations* (London, 1990).
20. Ibid., pp.3–30.
21. See, for example, Mass and Lazonick, 'British Cotton', pp.58–9.
22. T. Yui, 'Development, Organisation, and Business Strategy of Industrial Enterprises in Japan, 1915–35' in S. Yasuoka and H. Morikawa (eds.), *Japanese Yearbook on Business History*, Vol.5 (1988).
23. Suzuki, *Japanese Management Structures*, pp.15, 20–22, 26–9, 33–4; Morikawa, *Zaibatsu*, pp.105–14, 128–31, 144–59, 228–33; idem, 'Prerequisites for the Development of Managerial Capitalism: On the Basis of Cases in Prewar Japan', in K. Kobayashi and H. Morikawa (eds.), *The Development of Managerial Enterprise* (Tokyo, 1986); T. Yui, 'The Development of the Organisational Structure of Top Management in Meiji Japan', *Japanese Yearbook on Business History* (1984); Nakamura, *Postwar Japanese Economy*, p.18.
24. Suzuki, *Japanese Management Structures*, pp.1–12, 36–8; Morikawa, *Zaibatsu*, pp.46–55, 93–105.
25. See, for example, A. Gordon, *The Evolution of Labor Relations in Japan: Heavy Industry, 1853–1955* (Harvard, MA, 1988); and A.M. Whitehill, *Japanese Management Tradition and Transition* (London, 1991), pp.3–33.
26. Fruin, *Japanese Enterprise System*, pp.1–15.
27. H. Matsumoto, *Mitsui Zaibatsu no Kenkyu* (*Studies in the Mitsui Zaibatsu*) (Tokyo, 1979); Mitsui Bunko (ed.), *Mitsui Jigyo Shi* (*History of the Mitsui Business*), Vols.1–8 (Tokyo, 1972–80); S. Yasuoka, *Zaibatsu Keisei Shi no Kenkyu* (*Studies in the Formation of Zaibatsu Business*) (Tokyo, 1970).
28. Fruin, *Japanese Enterprise System*, pp.1–15.
29. Suzuki, *Japanese Management Structure*, pp.1–12.
30. See Gershenkron, *Economic Backwardness*.
31. Toyota in the 1980s joined the Mitsui group, but retains its operational freedom and financial independence.
32. See J.C. Abegglen and G. Stalk, *Kaisha: The Japanese Corporation* (New York, 1985).
33. Whatever their analytical faults, T.J. Peters and R.H. Waterman, *In Search of Excellence* (New York, 1982) and T. Deal and A. Kennedy, *Corporate Cultures: The Rites and Rituals of Corporate Life* (London, 1982) reviewed a number of US corporations, stating that their success depended on attention to human motivation and capability rather than on formal organisational systems.
34. See S.R. Clegg, *Postmodern Organisations Studies in the Postmodern World* (London, 1990).
35. K. Odaka, 'The Source of Japanese Management', in S. Durlabhji and N.E. Marks (eds.), *Japanese Business: Cultural Perspectives* (New York, 1989), pp.20–25; idem, *Japanese Management: A Forward Looking Analysis* (Tokyo, 1986) S. Durlabhji, 'The

Influence of Confucianism and Zen on the Japanese Organisation', in Durlabhji and Marks (eds.), *Japanese Business*, pp.57–8, 60–64, 68–72; J.C. Abegglen, *The Japanese Factory: Aspects of its Social Organisation* (New York, 1958); R.P. Dore, *Education in Tokugawa Japan* (Berkeley, 1965), idem, *Aspects of Social Change in Modern Japan* (Princeton, 1967); K. Taira, *Economic Development and the Labor Market in Japan* (Columbia, 1970); idem, 'Factory Labour and the Industrial Revolution in Japan', *Cambridge Economic History of Europe*, Vol.VIII (Cambridge, 1978); Whitehill, 'Japanese Management', pp.6–15; C. Nakane, *Japanese Society* (London, 1973); M. Morishima, *Why Has Japan Succeeded?: Western Technology and the Japanese Ethos* (Cambridge, 1989); and Y. Murakami, '*Ie* Society as a Pattern of Civilisation', *Journal of Japanese Studies*, Vol.10 (1984), pp.281–363.

36. See, for example, P. Berger, *The Capitalist Revolution* (London, 1987); H. Kahn, *World Economic Development: 1979 and Beyond* (London, 1979). See also M. Bond and G. Hofstede, 'The Confucius Connection: From Cultural Roots to Economic Growth', *Organisational Dynamics*, Vol.16 (1988), pp.4–21.

37. G. Hofstede, *Culture's Consequences: International Differences in Work Related Values* (London, 1980); idem, *Cultures and Organisations: Software of the Mind* (London, 1991).

38. M. Granovetter, 'Economic Action and Social Structure: the Problem of Embeddedness', *American Journal of Sociology*, Vol.91 (1985), pp.481–510.

39. See M. Weber, *The Protestant Ethic and the Spirit of Capitalism* (London, 1930).

40. See A.D. Chandler, *Scale and Scope: The Dynamics of Industrial Enterprise* (Harvard, 1990); H. Mintzberg, *The Structuring of Organisations*, (New Jersey, 1979).

41. A. Etzioni, *The Comparative Analysis of Complex Organisations* (London, 1961 and 1975).

42. See D.C. Dunphy, 'An Historical Review of the Literature on the Japanese Enterprise and its Management', in S.R. Clegg, D.C. Dunphy and S.G. Redding, *The Enterprise and Management in East Asia* (Hong Kong, 1986), pp.343–68.

43. M.J. Wiener, *English Culture and the Decline of the Industrial Spirit, 1850–1980* (London, 1983).

44. Chandler, *Scale and Scope*, pp.51–89.

45. Hannah, 'Scale and Scope: Towards A European Visible Hand', *Business History*, Vol.33 (1991), pp.297–309.

46. M. Albert, *Capitalism versus Capitalism* (London, 1993); J. Edwards and K. Fischer, *Banks, Finance, and Investment in Europe* (Cambridge, 1993).

47. Fruin, *Japanese Enterprise System*.

48. Ibid., pp.71, 110; Tokyo Shibaura Denki, *Toshiba Hyakunenshi* (Tokyo, 1977).

49. Mitsubishi Corporation, *An Outline of the Mitsubishi Enterprise* (Tokyo, 1942), p.2. Despite its purchase of the Nagasaki shipyard, Mitsubishi's interests were not predominantly industrial until 1917–18, when there was a rush to meet government orders and supply the markets lost by major combatants of the First World War.

50. C. Johnson, *MITI and the Japanese Miracle: The Growth of Industrial Policy, 1925–75* (Stanford, 1982).

51. P.A. O'Brien, 'Industry Structure as a Competitive Advantage: The History of Japan's Post-War Steel Industry', in C. Harvey and G. Jones (eds.), *Organisational Capability and Competitive Advantage* (London, 1992), pp.128–59.

52. Johnson, *MITI* pp.287–9; M.A. Cusumano, *The Japanese Automobile Industry: Technology and Management at Nissan and Toyota* (London, 1989), pp.22–3; M. Fransman, *The Market and Beyond: Cooperation and Competition in Information Technology in the Japanese System* (Cambridge, 1990), pp.286–7; D. Todd, *The World Electronics Industry (London, 1990)*. Fransman outlines MITI's lead in information technology research between 1948 and 1959, with the locus of activity moving to individual companies in the more mature markets of the 1960s, but switching to co-operative ventures in the 1970s. Nonetheless, relationships remain competitive, as they have been in electronics where state-sponsored, co-operative research and development has not

been notable historically. See also H. Patrick (ed.), *Japan's High Technology Industries: Lessons and Limitations of Industrial Policy* (Tokyo, 1986).

53. Even by 1970, the top nine *sogoshosha*, ranked according to turnover, accounted for 48 per cent of all exports and 63 per cent of all imports. See S. Yonekawa and H. Yoshihara, *The Business History of General Trading Companies: Historical and Comparative Perspectives* (Tokyo, 1988); and C.J. McMillan, *The Japanese Industrial System* (New York, 1989).

54. Morikawa, *Zaibatsu*, pp.35–9, 226–7; Suzuki, *Japanese Management Structures*, pp.46, 57.

55. Morikawa, *Zaibatsu*, passim.

56. It is worth noting that, of the 325 companies targeted for dissolution, action was taken against the very small figure of 18 concerns.

57. See also K. Matsumoto, *The Rise of the Japanese Corporate System: The Inside View of a MITI Official* (London, 1993).

58. G. Gamilton and M. Orru, 'The Organisational Structure of East Asian Companies' and T. Hattori, 'Japanese Zaibatsu and Korean Chaebol', in K.H. Chung and H.K. Lee (eds.), *Korean Managerial Dynamics* (New York, 1989), pp.39–50, 79–98; S.G. Redding and D.S. Pugh, 'The Formal and the Informal: Japanese and Chinese Organisational Structures', in S.R. Clegg, D.C. Dunphy and S.G. Redding (eds.), *The Enterprise and Management in East Asia* (Hong Kong, 1990), pp.153–67; R. Whitley, *East Asian Business Systems* (London, 1993).

59. Fuji, it should be remembered, was the successor to the old Yasuda *zaibatsu*.

60. Fruin, *Japanese Enterprise System*, p. 138.

61. See, for example, M. Marquadt and A. Reynolds, *The Global Learning Organisation: Gaining Competitive Advantage through Continuous Learning* (New York, 1994).

62. K. Azumi and C. McMillan, 'Culture and Organisational Structure', *International Studies of Management and Organisation*, Vol.5 (1975), pp.35–47.

63. See J.P. Womack, D.T. Jones and D. Roos, *The Machine That Changed the World: The Story of Lean Production* (New York, 1992), and Cusumano, *Japanese Automobile Industry*.

64. Gordon, *Evolution of Labor Relations in Japan*.

65. See K. Taira, 'Characteristics of Japanese Labor Markets', *Economic Development and Cultural Change*, Vol.10 (1961), pp.150–68; and *Economic Development and the Labour Market in Japan* (Columbia, 1970).

66. See also T. Shirai and H. Shimeida, 'Interpreting Japanese Industrial Relations', in J.T. Dunlop and W. Galenson (eds.), *Labor in the Twentieth Century* (New York, 1978), pp.242–83; and Y. Sugimoto, 'Japanese Society and Industrial Relations', in H. Shimeida and S. Levine (eds.), *Industrial Relations in Japan* (Melbourne, 1982), pp.1–20.

67. See T. Nakamura, *The Postwar Japanese Economy: its Development and Structure* (Tokyo, 1980), pp.15–16.

68. Fruin, *The Japanese Employment System*, pp.29–30.

69. The extent to which Japanese manufacturing in the aggregate now specialises in product differentiation as opposed to cost advantage is disputed in Y. Suzuki, 'The Competitive Advantage of Japanese Industries: Developments, Dimensions and Directions', in R. Fitzgerald (ed.), *The Competitive Advantages of Far Eastern Business* (London, 1994). See also M. Porter, 'The Competitive Advantages of Far Eastern Business: A Response', *Journal of Far Eastern Business*, Vol.1 (1994–95).

70. J.C. Abegglen and G. Stalk, *Kaisha: The Japanese Corporation* (New York, 1985).

The Role of Managerial Enterprise in Post-War Japan's Economic Growth: Focus on the 1950s

HIDEMASA MORIKAWA

Keio University

A specific form of business, the managerial enterprise, has made a significant contribution to the development of Japanese organisational capabilities and post-war economic growth. With comparatively few natural factor endowments, Japan's success has rested on the creation and maintenance of competitive advantages in technology and management; it has depended, consequently, on managerial structure. As Chandler has noted, managerial enterprises are firms in which representatives of the founding families or of financial interests no longer make top-level management decisions – where such decisions are made by salaried managers who own little of the companies' stock.[1] It is large businesses controlled by salaried managers which led and spurred Japan's post-war period of rapid economic growth. But this is a conclusion that leaves several questions unresolved. Was it the managerial enterprise only that promoted economic growth? What were the respective roles of entre-preneurial and family enterprise? Who were the salaried managers that controlled the top management of managerial enterprises? How do we explain the link between managerial enterprises and post-war economic growth? The development of managerial enterprise in the 1950s raises a number of critical issues, and these have to be evaluated if we are to understand the roots of Japanese economic success.

II

CHANGES IN THE ROLE OF PRESIDENT IN THE LARGEST
JAPANESE COMPANIES

Table 1 provides an overview of how managerial enterprise developed in Japan. First, four points in time are selected: 1930, 1955, 1975, and 1992. Next, the largest business enterprise in each major industry is shown.[2] For 1930, paid-up capital is used as the measure of the size of the enterprise, but, for the subsequent three periods, the measure is total assets. Then the president of the largest enterprise in each major

TABLE 1
THE DEVELOPMENT OF THE MANAGERIAL ENTERPRISE IN JAPAN

Presidents	1930	1955	1975	1992
A: Full-time				
Salaried managers promoted from within	3 (1)	35 (5)	41 (8)	49 (7)
Founders	8	3	3 (1)	3
Subtotal	11	38	44	52
B: Full-time				
Professional (non-company specific) salaried managers	4	3 (1)	3	2 (1)
Founder's family members	4	4	8 (1)	6 (1)
Former high-ranking bureaucrats(amakudari)	1	0	2 (1)	1 (1)
Major stockholders	1	0	0	0
Sent from bank or other financial institutions	0	2	1	1 (1)
Parent company's representatives	0	1	2	0
Salaried manager's heirs	0	1	2	3 (1)
Subtotal	10	11	18	13
C: Part-time				
Founder's family members	4	0	0	0
Former bureaucrats (amakudari)	5	3	3	0
Major stockholders	11	2	1	0
Sent from bank or other financial institutions	0	1	0	0
Parent company's representatives	2	0	0	0
Salaried manager's heirs	0	1	0	0
Subtotal	22	7	4	0
Total	43	56	66	65

Sources: Shogyo Koshinsho, *Zenkoku Shokaisha Yakuinroku* (*Company Directory*), 1930 edition; *Diamond-sha Kaisha Shokuinroku* (*Company Directory*), 1955, 1975, 1992 editions.

industry is classified into one of three groups: full-time (A and B) and part-time (C). Full-time presidents are sub-classified into salaried managers promoted from within and founders (grouped under A) and seven other types (all grouped under B). The B group includes professionals (non-company specific: they moved from company to company seeking salaries), founder's family members, former high-ranking bureaucrats (*amakudari*), major stockholders, representatives of banks and other financial institutions, representatives of parent companies, and salaried managers' heirs.

In the 1930s, a greater number of major Japanese business enterprises began to employ a chairman as well as a president. In 1930, 2.5 per cent of these companies had both a chairman and president. By 1943, that figure had risen to 19.1 per cent, and the ratio of enterprises using that system continued to rise, to 22.0 per cent in 1954, 48.5 per cent in 1974, and 64.2 per cent in 1991.[3] In cases where a business enterprise with a president of type A is in office with a chairman of type B or C, or when a type B president is in office with a chairman of type C, the control of type A or type B presidents is diluted. The number of such cases is indicated in parentheses. The trends are obvious. There was a growth in the number of full-time presidents. While part-time presidents led more than half of these business enterprises in 1930, their numbers dropped steadily, to the point that no part-time presidents could be found among the enterprises surveyed in 1992. Among the full-time presidents, it is type A presidents and particularly salaried managers promoted from within that accounted for this steadily growing share. Between 1930 and 1955, salaried managers promoted from within also gained significantly against other types of salaried managers, including professional managers, former high-ranking bureaucrats, and salaried managers' heirs. If the changes that the table shows in 1955 to 1992 can be described as quantitative, the changes that occurred between 1930 and 1955 were qualitative.

III

THE DEVELOPMENT OF THE MANAGERIAL ENTERPRISE AND
ENTREPRENEURIAL ENTERPRISE BETWEEN 1930 AND 1955

Why this major qualitative change in the nature of top management within major Japanese business enterprises and in the chief executive officers at the core of top management occurred is a question that requires further study. It is possible, however, to draw attention to the most important factors. The years before 1930 had seen a consistent trend towards the development of managerial enterprise. Table 2 makes it clear that large business enterprises with a relatively high proportion of salaried managers on their boards of directors (the highest management body in Japanese enterprises) became predominant over time. But, in 1930, only 42 of these major business enterprises had a majority of salaried managers on their boards of directors; that is only 28 per cent of the 158 enterprises examined.[4] (If *amakudari* managers are included, the figure would rise to 52 per cent.) In 1930, managerial enterprise in Japan was still in a period of transition.

Another factor is the impact of the Second World War. The military wanted a rapid build up of the armament industry in order to support the war effort, and it required that presidents of the companies affected

TABLE 2
THE RISE OF SALARIED MANAGERS IN JAPAN

Year	Enterprises	Number of Salaried Managers on Their Boards					
		0	1	≥2	≥2 but not more than half	More than half	Unclear
1905	75	47 (33)	22 (32)	5 (9)			1 (1)
1913	115	48 (39)	38 (39)	29 (37)			0 (0)
1930	158	15 (11)	27 (17)	113 (127)	71 (75)	42 (52)	3 (3)

Notes: Large business enterprises were defined according to the following criteria:
1905: Paid-in capital of Y1 million or more (for banks, Y2 million or more)
1913: Paid-in capital of Y1.5 million or more (for banks, electric power, and mining companies, Y3 million or more)
1930: Paid-in capital of Y10 million or more (for banks and electric power companies, Y20 million or more)
Figures in parentheses include *amakudari* managers.

Source: Shogyo Koshinsho, *Zenkoku Shokaisha Yakuinroku* (*Company Directory*), 1905, 1913, and 1930 editions.

should have considerable managerial experience and operational knowledge. It favoured full-time salaried managers who were promoted to the president's position from within an enterprise rather than part-time representatives of the owners. This preference chimed with the long-standing anti-capitalist sentiments of the military. The chief agent of change was the Munitions Companies Act (*Gunju Kaisha-ho*), which took effect in December 1943. This law required munitions companies to place a person in charge of production. He was charged with placing responsibility to the state before responsibility to his company. If a company failed to co-operate, the government assumed powers to make appointments.[5] In most cases, munitions companies named their presidents. Since, according to the government order, the person in charge of production was required to supervise the production and factory manager, a part-time president representing the owners could no longer do the job; nor, in fact, could a full-time president unless he was a director with detailed knowledge of the company's operations. As a result, the presidents of munitions companies had to be full-time salaried managers promoted from within.[6]

The dissolution of the *zaibatsu* under the post-war occupation was a third factor. The rise of the *zaibatsu*, or diversified enterprise groups exclusively owned and controlled by single families, was a distinctive feature of Japan's pre-war business history. Salaried managers promoted from within moved into the top management positions in the operating companies and in the holding companies that were the head corporations within the *zaibatsu* structure. By 1930, the *zaibatsu* had evolved into what could be described as managerial enterprises, apart from a few enterprises such as Yasuda and Asano. Yet even if the *zaibatsu*'s *de facto* top management were salaried managers promoted from within, those salaried managers were still, *de jure*, servants of the *zaibatsu* families. Top management could not completely ignore the views of the owners, and the influence of salaried managers promoted from within over policy and operations was constrained. The dissolution of the *zaibatsu* and the ending of founding-family control boosted the power and influence of salaried managers.[7]

A fourth factor was occupation land and tax reform, whereby property and inheritance taxes were increased and a tax on wartime profits was introduced. These reforms dealt a harsh blow to the pre-war propertied class and affected major shareholders in business enterprises, many of whom had exercised considerable influence over top management. As a result, the major shareholders or owner-family members lost ground to salaried managers in the top management of joint-stock companies.[8] The purges of businessmen who had co-operated in the war effort, another part of occupation policy, was a fifth factor. That had no conspicuous effect on the relative weight of salaried managers promoted from within in the top management of major business enterprises, but it did reduce the average age of higher level management. People in top positions, from the director level up, were dismissed and replaced by younger subordinates, and the average age of senior managers in major business enterprises was reduced by about a decade.[9] Even greater scope had to be given to salaried managers promoted from within, who had already increased their sway over top management. A sixth factor was the founding of many business enterprises, which seized the opportunities presented by immediate post-war circumstances: shortages, chaotic markets, and the loss of direction experienced by existing large businesses. These new enterprises included Honda, Sanyo Electric, Sony, Kawai Musical Instruments, Minebea, Mita, Amada, Toyo Sash, Wacoal, and Nippon Meat Packers, all of which were founded between the end of the war and 1955. Casio Computer and Daiei, the pioneer supermarket chain, had similar origins, though founded slightly later, in 1957. The successful entrepreneurial enterprises that were established during the war, so benefiting from expanded military demand, should be considered in the same category. These include Matsushita Electric Industrial, YKK, and YAMMAR. The founders of the thriving businesses that developed in 1930 to 1955 were owners, but, unlike the owner families and major shareholders of the pre-war period, they were not exclusively focused on the worth of their monetary assets. They were personally committed to the growth of their new businesses; their dynamic entrepreneurial activities energised the post-war Japanese economy. The founders listed within the type A presidents in Table 1 include many who established their companies between 1930 and 1955. These same founders were the fathers or elder brothers of the presidents who were family members within the type B group. In summary, it is clear that the years 1930–1955, and especially the decade from the end of the war to 1955, were critical for Japanese business history. In that period, managerial enterprises – particularly those in which salaried managers promoted from within played a dominant role – came to dominate Japanese industry. The post-war decade was clearly a time when many hands-on founders not only launched but also made successes of nascent entrepreneurial enterprises.[10]

IV

HOW DID TOP MANAGEMENT STRENGTHEN
ORGANIZATIONAL CAPABILITIES?

What effect, then, did the change in the composition of top management within large business enterprises that occurred between 1930 and 1955 have on economic growth in post-war Japan? In the past, many historians have argued that this period saw a rise in the managerial enterprise controlled by salaried managers, and that they were freed from the owners' preoccupation with monetary assets. These firms carried out aggressive three-pronged investments in management, manufacturing, and marketing as a means of gaining competitive advantage.[11] The result, it was concluded, was that Japan's industry developed and its economy grew. While that analysis is not wrong, it is one-sided. The term 'salaried managers' for those who led these managerial enterprises covers several types. They can be broadly categorised into three types that should not be lumped together: those promoted from within, professionals (non company-specific), and former high-ranking bureaucrats (*amakudari*). Furthermore, it was not just managerial enterprises led by salaried managers that contributed to industrial development and economic growth in the post-war period. We must not overlook the significant role played by entrepreneurial enterprises created by one type of owner-manager, the founder.[12] As a glance at Table 1 reveals, salaried managers promoted from within have accounted for an overwhelming share of the top management in leading large business enterprises from 1955 onwards. The next largest group of full-time top managers consists of founders and members of the founder's family, though they lost ground after 1930. In Table 1, members of a founder's family outnumber founders, but the contribution of the entrepreneurial founder, who built an enterprise from the ground up, is greater than that of the family members who follow him. It is erroneous to regard salaried managers as the sole agents of Japan's economic growth after the Second World War. We should clearly note the contributions of founders, second only to salaried managers promoted from within.

This view of post-war Japanese management raises a further question. Why did salaried managers promoted from within and founders succeed in strengthening the organisational capabilities of their enterprises and so make their signal contributions to Japan's industrial development and economic growth? At this point, an overview of theoretical perspectives will be useful. For a business enterprise to achieve a competitive advantage and growth, it requires organisational capabilities. The concept of 'organisational capabilities', as developed by Alfred D. Chandler Jr, refers to physical facilities such as factories, equipment, and testing centres as well as human skills.[13] It is noteworthy that Chandler did not include money as a category of organisational capability, since money itself can be meaninglessly hoarded or used for speculation. Money is not always invested in the furtherance of organisational capabilities: management must have a specific intention and reach a decision to invest. Although organisational capabilities consist of physical facilities and human skills, the second is more determinant. It is human skills that choose physical facilities, build them, and operate them. In their absence, physical facilities cannot exist. These critical human skills do not normally exist in isolation. The people who have them are organised and function in groups. Human skills are organised in different ways: sometimes a hierarchical, bureaucratic structure is found; sometimes a more flexible network structure permitting speedy, lively exchanges of information and human resources can be discovered. A skills network structure is better adapted to making the most effective use of human skills.[14] In either case, the organised group of human skills is the core of an enterprise's organisational capabilities, and the achievement of competitive advantage and growth depends on that core.

Human skills are of many types – technological, managerial, and operational – and people possess not one but a complex of skills. But human skills groups function at their best when the top management of a business enterprise has detailed information on the human skills groups they supervise and when the groups have confidence in the top management. What sort of top management can have detailed information on the human skills groups and receive their trust? The ideal would be either the founder or a salaried manager promoted from within. Salaried managers promoted from within are products of the skills group, where they received their start, their training, and their promotions to the top.[15] Founders, in the course of establishing and expanding an enterprise, must utilise their own capabilities to foster skills groups, and the growth of their enterprises is dependent on their emergence. Both salaried managers promoted from within and founders are ideally placed to feed back ideas and information between top management and skills groups, so building a relationship of mutual trust. By contrast, members of the founder's family, major shareholders, professional salaried managers, *amakudari* former bureaucrats, and representatives of financial institutions are in a far less favourable position, since they are all outsiders to the skills groups. If the top management is also part time, then their ties to the skills groups will be remote indeed. Between 1930 and 1955, and especially the ten years after 1945, top management consisting of salaried managers promoted from within or of founders became the dominant type among large Japanese business enterprises. Thanks to their connections with the groups of people who possessed the skills, and the contingent exchanges of information in a relationship of mutual trust, these top managers were able to enhance the organisational capabilities of Japan's business enterprises. They were able to invigorate the businesses that became the motive force behind industrial development and Japan's post-war economic growth.

V

THE START OF LARGE-SCALE, AMBITIOUS INVESTMENT

Between the end of the war and 1950, the Japanese economy experienced the despair and chaos brought by defeat, then inflation, black market speculation, the occupation's deflation measures, and bitter labour disputes. Those drastic changes inhibited the development of business activities. Consequently, it was in the 1950s that many large business enterprises actively invested and upgraded physical facilities. They began to make effective use of their organisational capabilities, with the network of skilled personnel at their core, to participate in fiercely competitive domestic and international markets. Around 1950, inflation was brought under control and radical, Communist-led labour disputes were defeated. An end to the occupation and a resumption of autonomy seemed possible in 1950, the year the Korean Conflict broke out. The resulting huge orders from the US Army and the so-called special procurements were the stimulus the economy needed.[16] Major Japanese business enterprises from 1950 onwards acted extremely energetically. It was as if they were trying to recover in one big push from the stagnation of the immediate post-war years, even though they had already been rationalising quietly. It is widely known that the leading business enterprises of the 1950s set themselves extremely un-realistic goals and challenged themselves to meet them. For instance, Japan's domestic crude steel production totalled 2.5 million tons in 1950. It was then that Kawasaki Steel, under the leadership of its president, Nishiyama Yataro, decided to build a large-scale integrated steel plant in Chiba with a productive capacity of 500,000 tons. The construction budget was Y16.3 billion, while Kawasaki Steel itself was capitalised at only Y500 million.[17]

Also in 1950, Bridgestone Tyre (now Bridgestone), founded by Ishibashi Shojiro, adopted a five-year modernisation plan which would focus production on the rayon-cord tyres pioneered by Goodyear in the United States. The total cost was Y1 billion, while Bridgestone Tyre's capitalisation stood at Y90 million in 1950. In that year, the company produced 360,000 tyres, while total domestic output totalled 1,130,000 tyres. Bridgestone's productive capacity was planned to reach 80 per cent of the national total when the five-year plan was completed in 1955. In 1951, when the market value of raw rubber inventories plummeted, the company recorded a massive loss of about Y3 billion. Ishibashi, instead of resigning as president, ordered that the five-year modernisation plan be continued.[18] In 1950, Tashiro Shigeki, the president of Toyo Rayon (now Toray) decided to introduce DuPont's Nylon 66 technology. The proposed initial royalties of Y1.08 billion ($3 million) outstripped the company's capital of Y750 million. Tashiro was not totally confident of his company's ability to mass-produce Nylon 66, but he pressed ahead, under the condition that the pre-paid royalties could be paid in instalments. As a result, Toyo Rayon underwent three hard years, but succeeded in becoming Japan's first mover in the nylon industry.[19]

Risk-taking enterprises like these were a striking feature of the Japanese economy in the 1950s. Ignoring the restrictions imposed by their managerial resources and the market environment, they set their sights ambitiously high. In conjunction with those goals, it was the improvement of organisational capabilities and company morale by top management that was critical. G. Hamel and C.K. Prahalad have given the name 'strategic intent'[20] to the type of ambitious deci-sions frequently made by Japanese enterprises after the War. Hamel and Prahalad neglected to discuss one important point: business enterprises do not succeed on sheer determination alone. In fact, since these managers pursued ambitious goals that transcended the limits of their managerial resources, their achievement required several other factors apart from strategic intent. First, high profits and rapid growth were achieved with existing operations. Kawasaki Steel had the steel output of its Kobe mill, Bridgestone had its tyre production based on existing technology, and Toyo Rayon had its rayon output. Second, the success in raising funds made an important contribution to managerial resources. These enterprises had relationships of trust with their banks and had striven in the past to accumulate internal reserves. Third, there existed within these businesses an inherent confidence that they could achieve a dramatic gain in human skills, that vital element of managerial resources. Top managers were assured of their ability because, as founders or salaried managers promoted from within, they understood their employees and held their trust. Armed with this confidence, they could persuade the banks. Because of the mutual trust between employees, managers, and banks, the managers were able to make massive and, at first glance, risky investments.

Kawasaki Steel's Nishiyama, for instance, brought in a number of engineers who had worked in the steel division of the old South Manchuria Railway. Returning to Japan after the War, they were lured to Kawasaki Steel by Nishiyama, their old high school and university friend. Moreover, he was confident of the skills which the younger engineers and blue-collar workers had attained over the years;[21] Kawasaki Steel's successful entry into the pig iron industry and the construction of a large integrated steel mill appeared feasible. Bridgestone's Ishibashi also had confidence in the company's engineers and operators. He believed that they could solve the knotty problems which would be created by the transplanting and operating of leading-edge production methods.[22] Toyo Rayon's Tashiro similarly anticipated that the technological and operational skills available in his company could be developed to a point where nylon of the required quality could be produced. Nishiyama was a salaried manager promoted from within; Ishibashi was a founder. Both were thoroughly familiar with the characters and abilities of their engineers, foremen, and other skilled workers, for their careers in the company were spent with them. Of course, their shared experiences and interdependent relationships led those skilled personnel as a group to trust their top managers and to take pleasure in being presented with ambitiously difficult problems and high expectations. The 'strategic intent' that was conspicuous in the business history of 1950s Japan is unintelligible unless the close relationship between top management and their skilled personnel groups is considered. It was, of course, top managers who were salaried and promoted from within or, alternatively, the founders who could achieve close relationships with those groups. The fact that they achieved a dominant position in the top management of large Japanese business enterprises between 1930 and 1955, and particularly between the end of the war and 1955, was a critical moment in post-war Japan's economic development.

VI

CONCLUSION

Large business enterprises in which salaried managers exercised substantial power from 1930 onwards and especially after the War played a major role in Japan's post-war economic growth. Managerial enterprises, in other words, powered the Japanese economy. It was their managers who undertook the commercial necessary in the 1950s, the take-off point for economic growth. Nonetheless, the argument is too general. To be exact, it was salaried managers promoted from within, not salaried managers in general, who controlled the top management of these pivotal managerial enterprises. They were able, by exercising 'strategic intent', to secure large-scale investment and modernisation programmes, because they had a vital asset: a close, trusting relationship with the groups of people within their companies who possessed the human skills, plus sufficient information about those skills to support their decisions and convince the banks. In the important sense that they too experienced a close, mutually supportive relationship between their top management and skills groups, entrepreneurial enterprises led by their founders were comparable to managerial enterprises. In any assessment of the important contributions to Japan's post-war economic growth, both managerial enterprises led by salaried managers promoted from within and, to a lesser extent, entrepreneurial enterprises must be included.

NOTES

1. A.D. Chandler Jr, 'The United States: Seedbed of Managerial Capitalism', in A.D. Chandler Jr and H. Daems (eds.), *Managerial Hierarchies: Comparative Perspectives on the Rise of the Modern Industrial Enterprise* (Cambridge, MA, 1980), p.14.
2. Due to considerations of space, the definitions of major industries and the names of the largest business enterprises have been omitted.
3. H. Morikawa, 'Nihon no Top Management', in H. Itami, T. Kagono and M. Ito (eds.), *Nihon no Kigyo System* (*The Japanese Business System*), Vol.3 (Tokyo, 1993), p.206.
4. Concerning the definition of large-scale managerial enterprise, see H. Morikawa, *Nihon Keiei-shi* (*Japan's Business History*) (Tokyo, 1981), p.20.
5. *Nihon Keizai Nempo* (*Quarterly Research on the Japanese Economy*) (Tokyo, 1943), pp.56–6.

6. T. Okazaki, 'Senji Keikaku Keizai to Kigyo' ('The Wartime Planned Economy and Private Companies'), in the University of Tokyo Social Science Institute (ed.), *Gendai Nihon Shakai (Modern Japanese Society)*, Vol.4 (Tokyo, 1991), pp.391–6.
7. H. Morikawa, *Zaibatsu: The Rise and Fall of Family Enterprise Groups in Japan* (Tokyo, 1992).
8. R. Miwa, 'Sengo Minshua to Keizai Saiken' ('Democratisation and Economic Reconstruction in Post-War Japan'), in T. Nakamura (ed.), *Nihon Keizaishi (Japan's Economic History)*, Vol.7 (Tokyo, 1989).
9. H. Miyajima, 'Zaikai Tsuiho to Shinkeieisha no Tojo' ('The Purges from the Business World and the Appearance of a New Age Range of Top Managers'), in H. Morikawa (ed.), *Businessman no tame no Sengo Keieishi Nyumon (Guidebook to the Postwar Japanese Business History for Businessmen)* (Tokyo, 1992), p.27.
10. H. Morikawa, *Nihon Keieishi (Japan's Business History)* (Tokyo, 1981), pp.167–8.
11. A.D. Chandler, *Scale and Scope: The Dynamics of Industrial Capitalism*, (Cambridge, MA, 1990), p.8.
12. Kikkawa, 'Sengo Nihon Keieishi no Shoten' ('The Focus of Post-War Japanese Business History'), in H. Morikawa (ed.), *Keieisha Kigyo no Jidai (The Age of Managerial Enterprise)* (Tokyo, 1991), pp.226–8.
13. Chandler, *Scale and Scope*, pp.35–7.
14. For the skills network structure, see M. Ito, *Gijutsu Kakushin to Human Network Gata Soshiki (Technological Innovation and the Human Network Type Structure)* (Tokyo, 1988).
15. H. Morikawa, 'The Education of Engineers in Modern Japan: An Historical Perspective', in H. F. Gospel (ed.), *International Training and Technological Innovations, A Comparative and Historical Study* (London, 1991), pp.143–5.
16. Keizai Kikaku-cho (Economic Planning Agency), *Sengo Keizaishi—Sokanhen (Post-War Japanese Economic History: Total Survey)* (Tokyo, 1957).
17. S. Yonekura, 'Sengo no Ogata Setsubitoshi' ('Large-Scale Fixed Investment in Post-war Japan'), in Morikawa (ed.), *Businessman no tame no Sengo Keieishi Nyumon*, p.99.
18. Bridgestone, *Bridgestone Tyre 50-nen Shi (50 Years of Bridgestone Tyre)* (Tokyo, 1982).
19. Toray, *Toyo Rayon Sha-shi (28 Years of Toray)* (Tokyo, 1954).
20. Hamel and C.K. Prahalad, 'Strategic Intent', *Harvard Business Review* (May–June 1989).
21. Tekko Shimbun-sha, *Tekko Kyojin Den: Nishiyama Yataro (Heroes of the Japanese Iron and Steel Industry: Yataro Nishiyama)* (Tokyo, 1971), pp.472–4, 628–9.
22. Ishibashi Shojiro Den Kanko Iinkai (Publishing Committee for the Biography of Shojiro Ishibashi), *Ishibashi Shojiro: Iko to Tsuiso (Shojiro Ishibashi: Posthumous Works and Reminiscences)* (Tokyo, 1978), pp. 348–9.

Kigyo Shudan: The Formation and Functions of Enterprise Groups

TAKEO KIKKAWA
University of Tokyo

It is widely accepted that the formation of enterprise groups after the Second World War founded a notable characteristic of the 'Japanese management system'. The report of the US–Japanese Structural Impediments Initiative Talks, published in 1990, focused on enterprise groups because they represented a typical example of Japan's closed markets and a cause of growing trade imbalance. The purpose of these groups and the nature of their contribution to industrial organisational capability is rooted in the period of their formation, the 1950s. During a time of uncertainty and forced reorganisation, Japanese companies established relationships with other firms which enhanced stability and protected their immediate futures. Interlocking share ownership brought a sense of security, allowed managers to control their own enterprises, and encouraged firms to think in terms of long-term growth rather than short-term profits. Formal inter-firm relationships enabled a capital-starved economy to finance joint ventures, which often required the importation of expensive foreign technology. Information could be more freely shared amongst mutually dependent allies, and transaction costs between firms were reduced. The objectives and advantages of inter-firm groupings altered over time, and these changes reflected developments within the Japanese economy and in the commercial and organisational needs of companies. The strengths of companies are determined by internal organisation, but also by external connections with suppliers, buyers, banks, government, and other firms and these can take the place of neo-classical market mechanisms. These institutional arrangements, both formal and informal, have been a notable aspect of the Japanese industrial system; something distinct from Anglo-American economies and one possible cause of competitive advantage and differential growth rates.

II

THE ROLE OF ENTERPRISE GROUPS

The word *keiretsu* generally refers to *kigyo keiretsu*, which is a vertical combination with one large company and a number of subsidiaries, and the Matsushita and Toyota groups are classic examples of this type. Enterprise groups, however, are called *kigyo shudan*, a horizontal combination amongst large companies. We will investigate the latter by looking at the six largest *kigyo shudan*, namely Mitsui, Mitsubishi, Sumitomo, Fuji Bank, Sanwa Bank, and Daiichi Kangyo Bank (or DKB). Each of these is a network of companies and they are all guided by a presidents' meeting. In 1991, these six groups – exclusive of their financial and insurance businesses – accounted for 13.0 per cent of Japan's total assets, 14.3 per cent of sales, and 15.2 per cent of net profits.[1] In other words, they comprised one-seventh of the Japanese economy. Why these enterprise groups were formed, what kind of functions they perform, and how they influenced decision-making in member companies are all questions which are central to our understanding of the Japanese economy and its business organisation.

It was in the middle of the 1950s, when the Japanese economy began to grow rapidly, that the formation of enterprise groups attracted attention. Mitsubishi Shoji (Mitsubishi Trading)[2] was reintegrated in 1954, Mitsui Bussan (Mitsui Trading)[3] in 1959, and the three Mitsubishi Jukos (Mitsubishi Heavy Industries) – Shin Mitsubishi Jukogyo, Mitsubishi Nippon Jukogyo, and Mitsubishi Zosen – were merged in 1964. These trends had wide-scale implications at home and abroad. At the time, they were strongly regarded as re-emerged *zaibatsu*, but they were different in many ways. The new *kigyo shudan* lacked parent corporations operating as holding companies, the influence of the *zaibatsu* family had disappeared, and member companies were independent.[4] A more important issue is why the *kigyo shudan* were formed after the war.

There is strong support for the view which regards enterprise groups as primary actors and member companies as secondary. Enterprise groups can be seen as independent decision-making bodies,[5] formed in order to dominate markets and make monopolistic profits. Therefore, the reason for their formation after the war is self-evident and the focal point of the argument shifts from the function of enterprise groups to their power. But this perception of enterprise groups as primary actors and member enterprises as secondary has been criticised by some scholars. They see the enterprise group only as an intermediary between company and market,[6] and members join in order to reduce transaction costs, exchange information, and share risks. Have those who advocate the predominance of member companies over enterprise groups answered the question of why they were newly formed after the war? Lacking an historical perspective, they do not distinguish between the original purpose of these enterprise groups (their fundamental function) and roles that were subsequently assumed (additional functions). There were differences, too, between groups formed at separate times, and the Mitsui, Mitsubishi, and Sumitomo Groups were founded earlier than the Fuji Bank, Sanwa Bank, and Daiichi Kangyo Bank Groups. In demonstrating the role of these *kigyo shudan*, the relationship between them and their member companies should be explicated, and historical contrasts between fundamental and additional functions must all be distinguished.

III

INTERLOCKING SHARE HOLDINGS

Why were enterprise groups newly formed after the Second World War? In other words, what was their fundamental function? As the case of Mitsui Fudosan (Mitsui Real Estate) illustrates, companies were seeking to interlock shareholdings and restore corporate stability.[7] Mitsui Fudosan was established in 1941 to manage the lands and buildings of the Mitsui families, who at the end of the war still owned all of the company shares. Because of the *zaibatsu* dissolution policy implemented under the occupation, the firm went public, and Mitsui Fudosan faced the greatest crisis in its history. The shares were sold in 1949, and the company tried to secure approximately 30 per cent of the shares with the aim of forestalling a third party who would trouble the controlling management. Mitsui Fudosan borrowed 100 million yen, and this sum was used to secure about 280,000 of the one million issued shares, each of which was worth 400 yen. Ownership by a company of its own shares contravened the Mercantile Law, and any attempt to establish another firm which might own the secured shares violated a clause in the Antimonopoly Law which prohibited holding companies. As a consequence, the representative director of Mitsui Fudosan, Chuji Yamao, its director, Kiyoshi Kusaka, and the president of several interested concerns, Hikosaburo Hayashi, assumed ownership of the shares as private individuals. From 1955, they called their arranged association 'Sanwakai', which means 'harmony of three'. Publicly, the shares were attributed to another company with whom Hayashi was closely involved. These shares were used as security for a loan which was unassociated with Mitsui Fudosan. The company was unable to receive profits from its hidden shares, and there was evident insecurity in an arrangement in which various financial institutions might recall the security on their loans. Mitsui Fudosan felt obliged to act. Until the mid-1950s, the active business development of Mitsui Fudosan was greatly constrained: outstanding loans did not benefit the company and crowded out the possibility of further fund-raising. But, from 1955, the new president, Hideo Edo, was intent on developing Mitsui Fudosan as a general real estate developer.

Following further capital issues in 1952, 1956, and 1957, the shares Sanwakai owned had increased to 2.84 million. Mitsui Fudosan decided to collect these shares and dissolve Sanwakai and, by mid-1959, 1.51 million shares had been redeemed. In addition, in July, Mitsui Fudosan doubled its capital through further allocations to the stockholders, and, at the same time, it offered 3.2 million shares to the public. It entrusted Nomura Shoken (Nomura Stock Co.) to sell the issue, and transferred the old Sanwakai shares to companies within the Mitsui Group. For example, Mitsui Bussan took 480,000 shares; Mitsui Ginko (Mitsui Bank) 320,000 shares; Nippon Seikojo (Nippon Steelworks) 200,000 shares; and Mitsui Kensetsu (Mitsui Construction) 150,000 shares. Mitsui Fudosan succeeded in stabilising its shareholdings by dissolving Sanwakai and making each company within the Mitsui Group a reliable and trusted shareholder. A major obstacle to growth was removed, and the company began to concentrate on a corporate strategy of reclamation work, housing projects, and skyscraper and office building. The Mitsui Fudosan example clearly shows the importance attached to the security and stability which had been lost with the dissolution of *zaibatsu*. Cross-ownership amongst enterprise member companies enabled the management of individual concerns to strengthen their position.

Although no other case was as dramatic as Mitsui Fudosan, companies within the former *zaibatsu* had similar experiences, and enterprise groups were newly formed after the war as a result of shareholdings being interlocked. Given that the fundamental function of enterprise groups was to stabilise ownership, the presidents' meeting of each group represented a gathering of leading shareholders. The presidents' meeting of the Sumitomo Group first convened in 1951; that of the Mitsubishi Group in 1954; that of the Mitsui Group in 1961, although executives higher than managing directors had met socially since 1950. The formation of *kigyo shudan* from amongst the three largest *zaibatsu* occurred at a relatively early date, because their dissolution greatly affected companies which sought to maintain a strong, internal control over shareholdings. But the predecessors to companies within the Fuji Bank, Sanwa Bank, and Daiichi Kangyo Bank Groups had been owned more openly, and they felt the consequences of *zaibatsu* dissolution to be less significant. They did not have the same need to form enterprise groups, and did not do so until the mid-1960s, when international capital transactions were liberated, and share prices stagnated as a result of the security crisis in 1965. Affiliated companies began to acquire cross-shareholdings and presidents' meetings – a gathering of new shareholders – were founded. The first within the Fuji Bank Group occurred in 1966, and that of the Sanwa Bank Group in 1967. On the other hand, the Daiichi Kangyo Bank Group did not establish a presidents' meeting until 1978 because Daiichi Ginko and Nippon Kangyo Ginko merged in 1971.

IV

THE ADDITIONAL FUNCTIONS OF ENTERPRISE GROUPS

The enterprise groups which were formed in post-war Japan with the aim of interlocking shareholdings and maximising company and managerial stability acquired additional functions and advantages. The constant contact and close links between members secured a level of trust which reduced transaction costs. The financiers of affiliated companies save on the cost of collecting information on borrowers, while member enterprises have a large and steady source of funds and investment. Trading and operational companies have the confidence to be heavily committed to other members, and joint action assists the attainment of economies of scale, the spreading of risks, and product diversification. They can, in addition, act collectively to reduce purchase and sales costs. While remaining independent, every company can strengthen its competitive power and commercial security through group membership.

The information that is exchanged formally and informally by executives through the presidents' meeting is one of the enterprise group's most important functions. Intelligence on markets, technology, and competitors, collected and shared by the member companies, diminishes uncertainty, and many investment decisions are accordingly facilitated. Primarily, the Japanese enterprise groups had a strong base in the intermediate goods industries, which sought economies of scale by investing in large-scale facilities. The role of information exchange within enterprise groups was critical to the growth of member companies in a period when their commercial future and strategies were linked to plant and equipment investment.

Japan was recovering from the war and facing industrially more advanced countries, and the *kigyo shudan* had an important part in the restoration of the economy and the furthering of competitiveness. This adjustment required the rationalisation of declining sectors and investment in growing industries, and this major shift was eased by the ability of member companies to share the costs and the risks. The decline of coal mining was a controversial social issue, and the allies of these concerns assisted with redundancies and, between 1954 and 1963, jointly funded the establishment of cement companies[8] as a replacement business. In the expanding petrochemical industry, member companies of a group jointly estalished ethylene plants. Risk sharing within enterprise groups converted Japan's industrial structure and hastened economic growth. The functions of reduced transaction costs, information exchange, and risk sharing are not unique to enterprise groups. Transaction costs can be lowered by companies that have long-term, stable transaction relationships, and the exchange of information and the sharing of risks occurs without the existence of enterprise groups. But the *kigyo shudan* are especially suited to the gaining of such advantages, and, within enterprise groups, they are secured through stabilised ownership and interlocking shareholdings.

V

THE COMPLEMENTARY ROLE OF GROUPS

However, are the advantages of enterprise groups so great that they act as single decision-making bodies with precedence over member companies? Yoshikazu Miyazaki believes enterprise groups to be dominant, and offers the petrochemical industry as an example.[9] Four companies in the late 1950s were authorised ethylene producers within the state's First Plan for the domestic petrochemicals industry.[10] Two of them were Mitsui Sekiyu Kagaku (Mitsui Petrochemicals), jointly established by member companies of the Mitsui group in 1955, and Mitsubishi Yuka (Mitsubishi Petrochemicals), founded by companies within the Mitsubishi group in 1956. In order to participate in the overseas development of petrochemicals in the 1970s, the Mitsui group established Iran Sekiyu Kagaku Kaihatsu (Iran Petrochemical Development) in 1971, and the Mitsubishi group founded Saudi Sekiyu Kagaku (Saudi Petrochemicals) in 1979. These were clear examples of *kigyo shudan* acting collectively, but there were contrary cases. The Sumitomo group was different to the Mitsui and Mitsubishi groups in two important respects. Sumitomo Kagaku (Sumitomo Chemicals), authorised by the First Plan to undertake the domestic production of petrochemicals, began manufacturing ethylene independently from other member companies in the Sumitomo group. Overseas, it also took independent action and after 1975 built a complex in Singapore. Following the Second Plan dealing with the domestic production of petrochemicals, drawn up in the early 1960s, Kasei Mizushima (Mizushima Chemicals) brought conflict between Mitsubishi Yuka and its own parent company, Mitsubishi Kasei (Mitsubishi Chemicals), when Mizushima began to operate an ethylene plant in competition with Mitsubishi Yuka. In 1965, the entry of Osaka Sekiyu Kagaku (Osaka Petro-chemicals) into ethylene production caused conflict between Mitsui Sekiyu Kagaku and Mitsui Kagaku (Mitsui Chemicals), which owned and controlled Osaka Sekiyu Kagaku. Consequently, severe rivalry occurred within the Mitsui and Mitsubishi groups, and joint invest-ment and industrial linkages in the petrochemicals sector extended beyond the boundaries of these formally linked companies after the Second Plan.

It is difficult to see how enterprise groups can be regarded as pri-mary actors. It is necessary to take a contrary view, which is to regard member companies as primary actors and enterprise groups as secondary. When there develops a gap between business plans and the organisational capacity of the company, the enterprise group has a role as an intermediary organisation that bridges this gap. Mitsui Kagaku and Mitsubishi Kasei had chosen not to enter ethylene manufacturing independently during the implementation of the First Plan for domestic production. They respectively established Mitsui Sekiyu Kagaku and Mitsubishi Yuka, and they required the backing of their enterprise groups. Through this decision, they overcame their individual inability to obtain funds and bear risks, and they enhanced their bargaining power. Negotiations with foreign enterprises and the Japanese govern-ment were central to the successful completion of the projects. Only enterprise groups could bid for the former military fuel facilities in Iwakuni and Yokkaichi, then being privatised by the government. In the event, Mitsubishi Sekiyu Kagaku bought the plant at Iwakuni; Mit-subishi Yuka secured the Yokkaichi works. The Mitsui and Mitsubishi groups also acted collectively in overseas projects, because individual members felt unable to bear the risks and wanted to maximise every source of information.

Sumitomo Kagaku, on the other hand, had proceeded on an independent basis because its planned ethylene facility at Niihama was not as complex as the other projects. Nor were privatisation of former military fuel facilities and negotiations with government relevant issues. In establishing its ethylene production company in Singapore,

Sumitomo Kagaku again acted without the assistance of the Sumitomo group, and it already had adequate information indicating the venture to be potentially profitable and realistic. Singapore was the third largest oil centre after Houston and Rotterdam, and naphtha could be obtained from Esso and Shell at globally competitive prices.[11] Sumitomo Kagaku's initial organisational capacity matched its business plans, and, even the cases of Mitsubishi Kasei and Mitsui Kagaku, the enterprises required assistance from their groups only during the First Plan for domestic production. As the potential of the petroleum industry became apparent to these interested parties, they chose to develop their own ethylene production facilities without assistance. Mitsubishi Kasei established Kasei Mizushima during the Second Plan for domestic production and Mitsui Kagaku continued to operate Osaka Sekiyu Kagaku independently. The role of the enterprise group was a complementary one, used by member firms to overcome the lack of organisational capabilities. In these cases, the member enterprises acted as decision makers and the enterprise groups were followers.

VI

THE LESSONS OF HISTORY

According to Chandler, the United States of the 1960s evinced tangible signs of a new trend in capitalism: companies moved into markets in which they had little competitive advantage, top management was separated from executives, operating units were sold in unprecedented numbers, the buying and selling of corporations developed into an established business, the financial objectives of portfolio managers influenced company strategies, and a market for corporate control was institutionalised.[12] Tadao Kagono and Takao Kobayashi offer another perspective, focusing on a shareholders' 'counter-revolution' that sought to reverse the earlier managerial revolution. 'In the United States, there were active discussions about management control until the middle of the 1960s, but their incidence significantly decreased in the latter part of the decade. The maximising of shareholders' profits became the dominant theme, and the increasing threat of take-over by conglomerates spearheaded a shareholders' "counter-revolution".'[13] According to Chandler, the new trend in capitalism spread to Europe, but Japan did not experience the phenomenon.[14] Japanese companies sustained and strengthened their organisational capability and attained competitive power at home and abroad. While the managerial revolution which gave control to salaried managers occurred in post-war Japan as it did in

Western industrialised countries, the 'counter-revolution' was not copied. As a consequence, Japanese companies were not forced to seek only short-term profits, and could extend their capabilities and competitiveness over the long term. By avoiding the shareholders' 'counter-revolution', major Japanese companies could invest and sustain high economic growth in the post-war period. The stabilising and interlocking of shareholdings within enterprise groups played a decisive role in avoiding the 'counter-revolution'.

Mitsui Fudosan, as a member company of an enterprise group, escaped the threat of take-over and short-termist managerial behaviour. The additional functions of transaction costs reduction, the exchange of information, and the sharing of risks, moreover, raised competitiveness and the growing market power of member companies. The enterprise group displayed the characteristics of economic rationality. The growth potential and competitiveness of their member companies existed in the companies themselves. As the case of the petrochemical industry demonstrates, the roles of enterprise groups are complementary.

Criticism of the *kigyo shudan* is rising in Western nations, which do not always understand their true objectives. Such critics ignore the damage inflicted on Western economies by the shareholders' 'counter-revolution', and they overestimate the influence of the Japanese enterprise group, which serves the purposes of its members. As the relationship between ownership structures in industry and rates of economic growth become better understood, Western attitudes may change. Nonetheless the contribution of the *kigyo shudan* to Japanese success is clear. In the late 1940s and 1950s, Japanese business underwent a period of adjustment to enforced, legal changes. Lacking capital, technology and comparable size, many companies overcame their own organisational deficiencies through the co-operative mechanism of the *kigyo shudan*. Cross-ownership enabled management to re-establish their control, and, freed of some of the profit pressures confronting Western companies, they could invest and maximise sales in a rapidly growing economy over the long term. The *kigyo shudan* was established as a useful part of Japanese business organisation; it contributed to Japanese economic success, and remains a source of competitive advantage.

NOTES

1. Toyo Keizai Shinposha (ed.), *1993 nenban Kigyo Keiretsu Soran* (*Year Book on Enterprise Groups for 1993*) (Tokyo, 1993), pp.29–31.
2. Following the dissolution of the *zaibatsu*, Mitsubishi Shoji was divided into about 160 companies in 1947.

3. Mitsui Bussan was similarly divided into 200-odd companies in 1947.
4. Y. Miyazaki, *Sengo Nippon no Keizai Kiko* (*The Economic Structure of Postwar Japan*) (Tokyo, 1966), p.222.
5. Miyazaki, *Keizai Kiko*, p.53.
6. K. Imai *et al.*, *Naibu Soshiki no Keizaigaku* (*Economics of Internal Structure*) (Tokyo, 1982), pp.126–30.
7. For more details on the case of Mitsui Fudosan, see Mitsui Fudosan Kabushiki Kaisha (ed.), *Mitsui Fudosan Yonjunenshi* (*Forty Year History of Mitsui Real Estate*) (Tokyo, 1985); T. Kikkawa, 'On the Rapid Growth of Mitsui Fudosan', *Aoyama Business Review*, No.12 (Tokyo, 1986), and idem, 'Kabunushi Anteika to Kigyo Seicho' ('Stabilisation of Shareholders and Growth of Enterprise'), *Aoyama Keiei Ronshu* (*Aoyama Journal of Business*), Vol.27 No.1 (Tokyo, 1992).
8. This is equivalent to the establishment of Mitsubishi Cement in 1954, of Mitsui Cement in 1963, and of Sumitomo Cement in 1963.
9. Miyazaki, *Keizai Kiko*, p.53.
10. For more details on the case of the petrochemical industry, see T. Kikkawa, 'Nippon ni okeru Kigyo Shudan, Gyokai Dantai oyobi Seifu' ('Enterprise Groups, Industry Associations, and Government in Japan'), *Keiei Shigaku* (*Japan Business History Review*), Vol.26 No.3 (Tokyo, 1991).
11. Sumitomo Kagaku Kogyo Kabushiki Kaisha, *Sumitomo Kagaku Kogyo Kabushiki Kaishashi* (*History of Sumitomo Chemicals*) (Tokyo, 1981), pp.659–60.
12. A.D. Chandler Jr, *Scale and Scope* (Cambridge, MA, 1990), pp.621–6.
13. T. Kagono, T. Kobayashi *et al.*, *Kyoso to Kakushin* (*Competition and Innovation*) (Tokyo, 1988), p.218.
14. Chandler, *Scale and Scope*, pp.622, 626–7.

The Formation of Distribution *Keiretsu*: The Case of Matsushita Electric

MASAHIRO SHIMOTANI
Kyoto University

The ongoing Structural Impediments Initiative, held between the United States and Japan since 1989, has proved to be a forum for reconsideration of the various economic systems that have contributed to Japan's rapid post-war growth and transformation into an economic power. Of these, the so-called *keiretsu* system has attracted the greatest attention. *Keiretsu* are the close, long-term business relationships established by large corporations with select groups of smaller firms, and they are linked through investment and the exchange of personnel. These *keiretsu* are an effective system of minimising transaction costs, and an efficiency gain that has contributed to Japan's economic success. But the system has often been criticised for excluding outside firms from markets and, more particularly, as a barrier to foreign firms entering the Japanese market. Although *keiretsu* relationships appeared in the 1930s, it was in the 1950s that they were rapidly consolidated. In the post-war years, larger corporations chose their trading partners in areas such as production and distribution, and set about forming close, long-term (and hence exclusive) business relationships. The *keiretsu* were a response to the intense competitive pressures which existed among Japanese firms; certainly, their primary purpose was not to exclude foreign firms. The *keiretsu* system resulted from corporate competition within the Japanese economy, and became established as a link between firms that was economically rational, and suited to Japanese-style management. As the Japanese economy grew and advanced globally, however, the system of *keiretsu* relationships began to be seen as an unfair barrier. In this paper, the case of Matsushita Electric Industrial (National/Panasonic) will be examined, with particular emphasis on the process by which its distribution *keiretsu* was formed.

II

THE MATSUSHITA KEIRETSU

The case of Matsushita Electric Industrial demonstrates fully the rationale of distribution or vertical *keiretsu*. Matsushita Electric Industrial

TABLE 1
THE PREWAR MATSUSHITA GROUP

Year	Employees	Total Sales
1918	25	
1922	40	180
1928	300	
1932	1,102	3,000
1935	2,874	8,870
1937	4,007	16,500
1939	6,672	28,100
1941	9,346	34,060
1943	14,061	46,730
1945	26,832	69,730

Notes: Sales figures are in units of Y1,000. Columns 2 and 3 include the employees and sales of subsidiaries.

Source: Matsushita Electric Industrial, *Sogyo 35 nenshi* (*The First 35 Years*) (1953). Also, Matsushita Electric Industrial, *Matsushita Denki 50 nen no ryakushi* (*A Survey of the 50 Year History of Matsushita Electric*) (1968).

(MEI), the core of the Matsushita Group, was founded in Osaka in 1918, and Table 1 indicates the rapid growth of a once small entrepreneurship. The company's record both parallels the expansion of the Japanese economy in general and reflects the expansion of the Japanese home appliance and electronics industry, which has a history of continuous product diversification. In 1933, the company decided to become the first Japanese enterprise to introduce a system of decentralised operating divisions, and Table 2 tracks the progress of Matsushita's rapid product diversification efforts. The process began with the creation of four divisions: Radio, Batteries & Lamps, Wiring Equipment, and Electric Heaters. Each division was an individual profit-centre, responsible for its own manufacturing and sales activities. In addition, each division was envisaged as a point of intimate contact between manufacturing and sales functions.[1] However, this system of operating divisions was short-lived; after two years, the company decided to spin off the original four divisions to create five new, wholly-owned subsidiaries. Two to three years later, several seperate sales subsidiaries were also created. This network of subsidiary companies formed the prototype for the Matsushita Group, originally known as the *Matsushita sangyodan* or Matsushita Group of Industries. The company's product diversification and sales network expansion were such that, by the time of Japan's defeat in 1945,

TABLE 2
MATSUSHITA'S PREWAR DIVERSIFICATION

1918	Various plugs
1922	Battery operated lamp
	More than ten products
1927	Electric iron
1928	Electric range
1929	Electric heater
1930	Radio
1931	Dry cell battery
	More than 200 products
1932	Cooker, generator lamp, speaker
1933	More than 300 products
1934	Small motor, electric blanket, foot warmer
1935	Industrial electric furnace, toaster, coffee maker
1936	Various light bulbs, fan, stand lamp, electric clock
1937	Storage battery, record player, dryer
	More than 2,000 products

Source: Matsushita Electric Industrial, *Matsushita Denki 50 nen no ryakushi* (*A Survey of the 50 Year History of Matsushita Electric*) (1968).

a total of 49 subsidiaries had been created or brought in through purchase or equity participation, although there were never as many as that at any one time. As manufacturing and sales companies were spun off from the core, the parent company (MEI) maintained control through stockholdings. The original single corporate entity of Matsushita was accordingly divided and managed as a large number of subsidiaries, operating within the Matsushita Group. The top management of each subsidiary retained responsibility for manufacturing and sales within their individual profit-centres, in the same manner as the predecessor operating divisions. Although the subsidiaries were legally separate corporations, important personnel and planning decisions required the prior approval of the parent company. Comptrollers of subsidiaries were always dispatched directly from MIE, and top management within the subsidiaries had no influence over these appointments. As strategy, personnel, accounting, and other functions were subject to control from above, the concept of the so-called 'autonomous' profit-centres worked within the tight limits imposed by MIE. While the Matsushita Group was composed of many subsidiary companies, in reality it operated as a single organic whole. An organisation divided into many operating sub-sidiaries but functioning as a single unit could be described as a 'corporate group'.[2] The roles of the subsidiaries within it can be essentially divided into two. The first concerns the manufacture of a product which amounts to a diversification away from the parent company's main line of business. The second type of objective is to provide parts, materials, reprocessing, sales, or other services that vertically support the parent company. This kind of corporate group organisation, created out of satellites spun off from the main company, is hardly limited to Matsushita; it was adopted by many Japanese firms in the 1930s. Because of rapid economic growth during that decade, the progress of diversification and vertical integration brought organisational difficulties and inefficiencies to many companies. The corporate group and the subsidiaries proved to be an effective strategic response.

While the Matsushita Group had developed within the home appliance and electronics industry, economic controls instituted from the late 1930s and increasingly intensified during the Second World War stringently curtailed civilian demand for household durables, and almost all production was shifted to military purposes.[3] While some formerly existing units – notably radio and radar – became recipients of inordinate amounts of resources, the company had to manufacture other military products unconnected with former lines of business. Faced with incentives and pressure from the military, Matsushita began to make an array of war products including weapons parts and wooden aircraft. During the conflict, the military forced many small and medium sized producers to become subcontractors to certain large companies. At the time, these subcontractors were called 'co-operative producers', and Matsushita's five main production subsidiaries were allotted 487 of these smaller enterprises. This system of subcontracting, which played an important role in Japan's post-war rapid economic growth, came into existence during the period of wartime controls. Defeat dealt a heavy blow to industrial production, and the problems of Japanese companies were exacerbated by the break-up of the *zaibatsu* and other large companies, a policy imposed by the American General Headquarters.[4] Matsushita was forced to divest some of its subsidiaries, and these became independent. In response to this dislocation, the company reverted in 1950 to the operating division system, and three divisions were formed in an attempt to refocus the business.

In spite of these difficulties, post-war Japan offered a wider range of opportunity to the home appliance and electronics industry and Matsushita. Table 3 reveals the company's swift growth between 1950 and 1960 in terms of sales and employees. Even more indicative is an

TABLE 3
MATSUSHITA'S GROWTH IN THE 1950s

Year	Employees	Total Sales
1950	4,049	
1952	6,092	9,050
1954	8,924	17,460
1956	11,788	31,180
1958	16,509	53,810
1960	23,350	105,480

Note: Sales figures are in units of Y1 million.

Source: Matsushita Electric Industrial, *Sogyo 35 nenshi* (*The First 35 Years*) (1953). Also, Matsushita Electric Industrial, *Matsushita Denki 50 nen no ryakushi* (*A Survey of the 50 Year History of Matsushita Electric*) (1968).

increase in the number of divisions, which, organised along product lines, resulted from the birth of new lines in the first three divisions. There were a total of 15 divisions in 1956; 36 in 1964; 59 in 1972; and 65 in 1974.[5] Naturally, the rise in the number of decentralised divisions invited administrative difficulties and inefficiencies, just as Matsushita had experienced in pre-war years. Experiments were made with group related divisions under the aegis of several over-arching operations centres, but this solution tended to stifle the activities of supposed autonomous units. Finally, it was decided to spin off the numerous divisions into a number of outside subsidiaries. The core of the current Matsushita Group, as shown in Table 4, is made up of MEI and its 11 main subsidiaries, five of which (in the lower part of the table) were not originally Matsushita companies; they were brought in from outside. The other six subsidiaries (in the upper part of the table) were formerly parts of the parent company. Two of these were externalised as early as the 1950s, and the other four were spun off in the 1970s. These six subsidiaries are comprised of 25 former divisions, however, so that, despite their nominal independence, they function as extensions of the parent. Another important development within the Matsushita Group was its vigorous overseas expansion. The first such sales subsidiary, American Matsushita Electric, was founded in 1959, while the first production subsidiary was National Thai, established in 1959. International subsidiaries were subsequently created one after another, with 25 being founded between 1961 and 1970, 60 between 1971 and 1980, and 76 between 1981 and 1990. The creation of domestic sales subsidiaries also proceeded rapidly, and the modern Matsushita Group,

TABLE 4
CORE SUBSIDIARIES OF THE MATSUSHITA GROUP (1993)

	Established	Capital	MEI%	Sales
Matsushita Electronics	1952	410	65.0	4,667
Matsushita Communication Industrial	1958	223	57.0	4,578
Matsushita Electronic Components	1976	230	98.7	3,820
Matsushita Housing Products	1977	60	100.0	1,684
Matsushita Industrial Equipment	1977	30	100.0	na
Matsushita Battery Industrial	1979	105	97.6	2,001
Matsushita Refrigeration	1972*	119	51.8	2,030
Kyushu Matsushita Electric	1955	254	52.0	3,470
Matsushita Seiko	1962*	121	59.0	949
Matsushita Graphic Communications	1970*	15	60.0	825
Matsushita Kotobuki Electronics	1969*	79	57.7	2,729

Notes: Capital and Sales figures are in units of Y100 million. Asterisk indicates year of company name change.

Source: MEI Annual Reports.

through its dual strategy of spinning off subsidiaries and internationalisation, has grown to a huge aggregation of some 670 manufacturing, sales, and service companies.

III

MATSUSHITA'S DISTRIBUTION *KEIRETSU*, 1918–1945

The formation of Matsushita's distribution keiretsu played an important part in the company's swift expansion, both before and after the Second World War. Refined upon its reintroduction in the 1950s, the prototype for this distribution *keiretsu* is to be found in the 1930s. Matsushita supplied home appliances and electronics between 1918 and 1937, the subsequent implementation of war-time controls curtailing the output of non-military products. During this 20-year period, the company actively built up its distribution *keiretsu*.[6] Its formation proceeded with the establishment of the company's regional sales offices (branches) and, under them, a network of contracted wholesalers/distributors and retailers. The first sales office or branch was established in Tokyo in 1920. Then, with the expansion of home appliance and electrical goods markets in the late 1920s and early 1930s, branches were opened in main cities such as Fukuoka, Nagoya, Osaka, and Sapporo, and in provincial centres such as Sendai and Kanazawa. The branch network was even expanded to the imperial colonies of Taiwan and Korea. The early 1930s was a period of rapid growth and consolidation in manufacturing and sales capability. The number of managerial employees topped 200, as did the number of products. Factory operatives soon numbered more than 1,000, working in ten different plants. The various sales branches were allocated carefully defined sales areas of the country, and they oversaw a network (*keiretsu*) of wholesalers and retailers which extended even to the most remote parts of Japan. A distinction was drawn between markets, namely large-scale users like corporations and government departments, and the 'general market' of individual consumers. The branches, under the direction of Matsushita's home office marketing division, undertook sales activities aimed at both these markets. In the early 1930s, the company set up an internal Trading Division which became the Export Division in 1934. Matsushita Electric Trading Ltd, a subsidiary company created to take over all export-related business, was established in the following year, and it handled Matsushita exports until 1988, when it was re-absorbed into the parent, MEI. Matsushita's sales organisation, essentially a sales network controlled by a central marketing office, was superseded by the introduction of operating divisions in 1933 and by the creation of wholly-owned subsidiaries in 1935. A marketing section was established in each division or subsidiary, and the company's single marketing division was dissolved. The formerly centralised direction of the sales function was transformed into a decentralised structure organised by the various operating units. The new system allowed the autonomous operating divisions and subsidiaries to co-ordinate sales and manufacturing activities better, so meeting the needs of their respective markets more efficiently. The full development of decentralised selling was cut short, however, by the introduction of wartime economic controls.

One critical factor in the implementation of Matsushita's branch network in the 1930s was the hierarchical ordering of existing wholesalers and retailers into the company's distribution *keiretsu*. While Matsushita had been a comparatively small enterprise, it could rely on existing distributors and shops. But upon the release of its new battery-operated bicycle lamp in 1923, the company paid for newspaper advertisements seeking a wider group of distributors. As subsequent products such as an electric iron, an improved bicycle lamp, and an electric heater were introduced, the distributorship system was refined in the late 1920s. At first, contracts involved little more than a handshake or bow, but formal written agreements were instituted in 1929. With the introduction of radios and dry cell batteries in the early 1930s, Matsushita achieved unprecedented sales growth, and many established wholesalers expressed their desire to trade with the company. Wholesalers of the period typically handled competing items from several manufacturers, and the same was true for distributors of Matsushita products. But, in

1932, 'in order to concentrate attention on the sales of Matsushita products', and 'to promote deeper understanding of Matsushita's managerial and marketing aims',[7] the company sought exclusive deals with distributors. From 1933, incentives were offered to co-operating wholesalers and a 'dividend linked reserve fund' was established. Matsushita reserved three per cent of each exclusive distributor's monthly purchases, and this money was rebated to the distributors in the form of semi-annual dividend payments linked to Matsushita's financial performance.

The construction of the national branch network was accompanied by an ambitious effort to form an exclusive sales network of distributors and retailers under the supervision of the branches. But it was characteristic of Matsushita's marketing approach that the company also sought to bypass many wholesalers and establish direct links with retailers. According to contemporary comments of the founder, Konosuke Matsushita, 'The future will see manufacturers shaping the market. It should be the decision of the manufacturer as to how the market should be, how the sales network should be established within the market, and in what form sales should take place'. An important example of this policy was the publication from 1927 of the *Matsushita Denki Geppo* or *Matsushita Electric Monthly Bulletin*, aimed specifically at retailers. The opening issue stated that, 'Until now, there has been no forum for the two sides [Matsushita and its retailers] to meet, and it has been difficult to achieve sufficient recognition and understanding, but from here on we wish to deepen mutual understanding through close contact. We wish for you to present your opinions unreservedly'.[8] Matsushita was very aggressively approaching retailers, the tail-end of its distribution system, at the potential cost of traditional wholesalers. Publication of the *Bulletin* was suspended during the war, but it was replaced by the monthly *National Shop* in 1947.

The establishment in 1935 of the 'Associated Store' system represented further '*keiretsification*' of the sales system. It was designed as a means of rescuing distributors and retailers from the intense competitive discounting or 'sales war' which occurred in the early 1930s. The system reflected its motto of 'living together, prospering together', and it sought to secure a stable flow of sales for manufacturer, distributor, and retailer alike. Distributors identified the main retailers with whom they traded and registered them as 'Associated Stores'; registered retailers were to receive goods only from the one distributor. The policy transformed retailers into a series of smaller *keiretsu* operating under the aegis of distributors. Distributors secured their interests, and the stabilisation of market relationships enabled retailers to focus on customer service and increased sales, as opposed to bargaining over the best wholesale price. According to reports from distributors, Matsushita paid twice-yearly 'thanks dividends' to each 'Associated Store', the sum being determined according to retail sales. Such stores quickly appeared across the country, and there were more than 10,000 by the end of 1941. Yet Japan was already geared for war, and Matsushita's system of distribution *keiretsu* was almost completely dismantled under wartime conditions. It was not until after the conflict that actual results from the system were to be seen.

IV

MATSUSHITA'S DISTRIBUTION *KEIRETSU*, 1945–60

For several years after 1945, wartime destruction and the various restrictions enacted by the US administration hindered the rebuilding of manufacturing operations and the distribution *keiretsu* at Matsushita. The 1950s also saw the development of sales companies which were to become the new nuclei of distribution *keiretsu* in the post-war home appliance and electronics industry.[9] A number of new home appliance and electronics manufacturers were founded after the War, although most small makers went bankrupt during the deflation of 1949. The industry began to recover in the early 1950s and growth was led by those manufacturers who had survived the recent deflation. The procurements boom sparked by the Korean War in 1950 gave the whole Japanese economy a needed impetus. The refrigerator, the black and white television, and the washing machine – popularly known as 'the three jewels' – joined the radio as major products, and, as shown in Table 5, their production expanded quickly. Civilian radio broadcasts were permitted from 1951, and 1953 became known as 'year one of the home appliance and electronics era' in commemoration of the start of television broadcasting and in reference to the Japanese imperial dating system. In the midst of this boom, rivalry among home appliance and electronics makers intensified. Contributing to this competitive atmosphere was the entry of several heavy electrical equipment makers into the home appliance and electronics market during the 1950s. They enlisted the co-operation of foreign manufacturers: Toshiba paired off with General Electric of America, Hitachi with RCA, and Mitsubishi Electric with Westinghouse, bringing in large-scale capital, technology, and marketing muscle. As a result, the weight of home appliances and electronics in the total production of electrical equipment doubled between 1955 and 1960, rising from 20 per cent to 40 per cent.

TABLE 5
PRODUCTION FIGURES FOR THE JAPANESE HOME APPLIANCE AND ELECTRONICS
INDUSTRIES, 1955–60

Year	Total Value of Production	Black and White Televisions	Refrigerators	Washing Machines
1955	402	137,000	31,000	461,000
1956	725	312,000	81,000	754,000
1957	1,184	613,000	231,000	854,000
1958	1,699	1,205,000	415,000	988,000
1959	2,765	2,872,000	549,000	1,189,000
1960	3,726	3,578,000	908,000	1,529,000

Note: Total value of production figures are in units of Y100 million.

Source: Y. Okamoto (ed.), *Waga kuni kaden sangyo ni okeru kigyo kodo* (*Corporate Behaviour in the Japanese Home Appliance and Electronics Industries*) (1973).

Matsushita itself established close links with Philips in 1952, and its Central Research Laboratory was founded in the following year with the mission of fostering basic, production-related, and design research activities. Table 6 shows changes in market shares of black and white televisions for the major manufacturers of the 1950s. While there were a total of 32 makers in 1956, this number fell to 19 by 1960 and to ten by 1962. In order to retain its competitive position, Matsushita had to rebuild and strengthen its distribution *keiretsu*.

An internal marketing division was re-established in December 1945, and, in the following year, sales offices or branches were re-opened in seven major cities, including Tokyo, Osaka, Nagoya, and Hiroshima. A network of sub-branches was founded in 1949, and, as can be seen in Table 7, it expanded quickly. The country was divided into a number of regions, each of which was covered by a given branch or sub-branch. When the operating division system was re-established in March 1950, the internal marketing division was abolished and the various sales offices were assigned to the new divisions. Nevertheless, MEI continued to exert control over general marketing efforts.

The distributor system re-emerged as early as 1946, but contracts were only offered to those 'selected distributors with strong sales capabilities and a high degree of co-operativeness with our company'.[10] The *Nashonaru Kyoei Kai* or National Co-operative Prosperity Association was formed in 1949, and, through it, Matsushita's regional branches promoted contacts and exchange among distributors. The Association's first national convention was held in 1950, when membership stood at 240. By 1955, this number had risen to 580 (see Table 7), and, while many members originally handled the products of other manufacturers, they gradually switched to exclusive distributorship status. The National

TABLE 6
MONTHLY TELEVISION PRODUCTION AND MARKET SHARES (%)

	1956 (32 companies)		1957 (22 companies)		1958 (17 companies)		1959 (18 companies)		1960 (19 companies)	
	TVs	%	TVs	%	TVs	%	TVs	%	TVs	%
Matsushita	5,610	17.8	8,880	17.0	19,510	19.5	50,130	19.6	50,550	18.1
Sanyo	2,520	8.7	4,040	7.7	10,500	10.5	30,230	11.8	31,340	11.2
Hayakawa	5,140	17.7	7,120	13.6	11,830	11.8	34,210	13.4	28,000	10.0
Yaou	3,140	10.8	5,060	9.7	7,620	7.6	20,810	8.1	18,320	6.6
Columbia	1,000	3.4	2,440	4.7	3,990	4.0	10,630	4.2	9,570	3.4
Victor	720	2.5	2,030	3.9	3,970	4.0	11,230	4.4	5,820	2.1
NEC	180	0.6	340	0.7	1,330	1.3	5,910	2.3	11,570	4.1
Toshiba	5,000	17.2	9,920	19.0	20,390	20.3	41,910	16.4	50,950	18.3
Hitachi	450	1.6	4,000	7.7	12,000	12.0	28,740	11.2	43,810	15.7
Mitsubishi	3,650	12.6	5,170	9.9	6,580	6.6	18,080	7.1	24,130	8.7

Note: Output numbers indicate television production in the month of August for each given year.

Source: Y. Okamoto (ed.), *Waga kuni kaden sangyo ni okeru kigyo kodo (Corporate Behaviour in the Japanese Home Appliance and Electronics Industries)* (1973).

TABLE 7
MATSUSHITA'S SALES CHANNELS

	Branches	Sub-branches	Distributors (Wholesalers)	Sales Companies	Associated Stores (Retailers)
Dec. 1949	6	4	240		6,000
May. 1951	7	4	240	3	31,150
July 1952	8	20		5	33,000
Nov. 1953	8	27	250		30,000
Nov. 1954	8	36	560		30,000
Nov. 1955	13	39	580		30,000
Nov. 1956	13	44	580		40,000
Nov. 1957	13	42	550		40,000
May. 1958	13	26	381	72	40,000
Nov. 1958	13	18	367	88	40,000
Nov. 1959	13		226	106	40,000
Nov. 1960	15		210	106	40,000

Source: I.S. Son, 'Kodo seichoki ni okeru kaden ryutsu kozo no henka' (Changes in the Distribution Structure of the Home Appliance and Electronics Industry during the Period of Rapid Economic Growth), *Keizaigaku kenkyu (Economics Research)*, Vol.35 (1992).

Monthly Finance Ltd was created in 1951, and, organised through the regional branches, it originally focused on the company's main product, the radio. Each regional unit was jointly capitalised by Matsushita and its distributors, and, by the mid-1950s, there were some 30 of these finance companies. Other high-priced items were eventually made eligible for instalment financing.

In addition to consolidating its wholesaler network, the company also began to '*keiretsify*' its retailers. In 1949, the 'Associated Store' system was resuscitated, and, at first, it was organised along product lines, including radios, light bulbs, and batteries. In case of radios, a retailer was automatically registered as an 'Associated Store' when it returned ten or more 'Profit Sharing Coupons', one of which was attached to every radio. Registration entitled a retailer to the *Associated Store Report* and a variety of other information from Matsushita. Linked retailers received a semi-annual sales promotion payment, depending on the number of coupons submitted. The number of 'Associated Stores' grew from an initial figure of 6,000 to some 40,000 by the end of the 1950s. Alongside the re-establishment of 'Associated Stores', another organisation known as the National Association was founded. It sponsored sales technique study-groups and technical training presentations, as well as factory tours and other events in order to promote co-operation and under-standing among manufacturer, distributor, and retailer. The 'Associated

Store system', it was said, 'links Matsushita Electric with retailers all over the country, and the National Association is a distributor-centred organisation which seeks to promote exchange and close relations on a regional basis between retailers and distributors'. With the proliferation of new products, the Associated Store system could no longer be managed along individual product lines, and, in 1952, a new system that dealt with all retail products was instituted. Profit Sharing Coupons reflecting wholesale prices were attached to each item, and, when an agreed number of coupons had been collected, the shop was registered as a National Associated Store. A list of the top selling stores was circulated on a regular basis. The system encouraged each member retailer to handle a broad range of products and it allowed Matsushita to tabulate and analyse regional and product market data. It enabled Matsushita to consolidate its distribution *keiretsu* at the retail level, and it became 'our company's main [retail] sales system'.[11]

In 1957, the former National Association was reorganised as a network of regional National Store Associations, and the new organisation put special emphasis on improvements in the management, sales ability, and technical capabilities of its retailers. Originally, there were 110 associations consisting of 4,300 Associated Stores; by 1958, there were 248 National Store Associations comprising 10,300 Associated Stores. A National Shop system was also started in 1957, and, selecting only those Associated Stores with proven capabilities and high exclusivity, it was designed to foster an even higher level of commitment. National Shops were to sell only Matsushita products and, in addition to the usual benefits, they received subsidies for shop layout, fittings, signs and advertising materials, as well as extra cash bonuses. Their number grew from 925 in the initial year to 2,715 by the end of 1958. Consequently, Matsushita was able to rank its many retail outlets and solidify its retail *keiretsu* of exclusive dealers. The basic pattern for Matsushita's distribution *keiretsu* had been moulded before the war; the post-war period brought in the main reformation and refinement. Yet the sales companies were an entirely new development. From 1955, the Japanese economy entered a period of rapid growth, and Konosuke Matsushita responded in 1956 with his Five Year Plan. It called for sales to be increased from Y22 thousand million (billion hereafter) to Y80 billion, for capital to expand from Y3 billion to Y10 billion, and for the number of employees to rise from 11,000 to 18,000, all by 1960. In the event, these goals were surpassed. Sales, for example, were Y105.4 billion by 1960. But this achievement in the face of fierce competition had required major improvements in the sales organisation, and the establishment of the sales companies from 1957 were designed for this very purpose.

Even in 1936, a passage from *Matsushita Denki no Keiei Seishin* or *The Spirit of Matsushita Electric Management* reads: 'The maker is the factory of the distributor, and the distributor is a branch of the maker'. On his famous country-wide tour of distributors, just after the war, Konosuke Matsushita is reported to have said that, 'In order to aim for future prosperity, the distributors and Matsushita Electric must be even as one in body and spirit'. But he is also known to have remarked: 'It is clear that distributors managed in a personal and traditional style will not be able to keep up with the changing needs of the age'.[12] When the arrival of the former heavy electrical equipment manufacturers in the mid-1950s intensified competition in the home appliance and electronics industry, market stability was lost to cut-throat pricing regardless of costs. Matsushita thought about the long-term implications:

> In order to carry out wholesaler functions effectively, systematic improvement of capital availability, marketing capability, product knowledge, and technical service ability are urgently required, as are the strengthening of managerial ability and the modernisation of management control systems.[13]

The sales companies ensured an effective *keiretsu* network. Capital participation by Matsushita allowed it to become 'one in body and spirit' with the distributors. As can be seen in Table 7, some sales companies had been created in the early 1950s, but in 1957 the system was adopted throughout the country. In principle, there was to be one joint Matsushita-distributor sales company for each area. In most cases, management was the responsibility of the distributor, but, occasionally, managers were sent in from Matsushita. With the establishment of these sales companies, the numbers of branches and sub-branches could be correspondingly reduced. By funding its existing but separate main distributors, Matsushita achieved an even tighter grip on its distribution *keiretsu*. At the time, other makers were building up their own *keiretsu* organisations, but, as indicated in Table 8, because Matsushita started its network first, it gained first-mover advantages by incorporating the most valued distributors. This enhancement to capability was a major key to Matsushita's overall success during this period of rapid economic growth.

V

KEIRETSU DISTRIBUTION AND MARKETING

The establishment and maintenance of distribution *keiretsu* can be widely observed in Japan, particularly in the consumer goods industries,

TABLE 8
DISTRIBUTION *KEIRETSU* OF OTHER MANUFACTURERS

Company	Linked Retailers	Established
Toshiba	Mazda Link Stores	1956
	Toshiba Stores	1958
Hitachi	Hitachi Chain Stores	1957
Sharp	Friend Shops	1958
Sanyo	Sanyo Superstores	1959
Mitsubishi	Diamond Stores	1960

Source: Kaden Seihin Kyokai (Home Appliance and Electronics Products Association), 'Waga kuni kaden ryutsu kiko no hatten to hensen' ('The Development and Transition of the Japanese Home Appliance and Electronics Industry') (1984).

but Matsushita was both a model for and a driving force in their formation. Distribution *keiretsu* were a response to intense competitive pressures, and, through them, stability was re-imposed on the marketplace. Through their *keiretsu* networks, manufacturers could control prices, and they obtained a system for collecting valuable consumer information. In the 'keiretsification' of external wholesalers and retailers, manufacturers ranked distributors hierarchically and, through incentives, encouraged exclusivity. The organisation of various 'associations' and the provision of information, training, and monetary assistance solidified the formation of close business relations. Finally, manufacturers sought to invest in their distributors, forming in some cases joint sales companies. The needs of manufacturers for market share and stable prices, then, coincided with the needs of weak wholesalers and retailers for protection from price wars. Despite intense competition in the post-war period, manufacturers avoided price competition by focusing on quality, technology, and promotion. But from the 1970s, the *keiretsu* system began to break down as 'non-*keiretsu*' large-scale stores expanded. Home appliance and electronics distribution channels, which had once consisted only of *keiretsu* stores, were challenged by large independent retailers. Manufacturer-controlled prices invited resistance from consumers. The distribution *keiretsu* contributed to 'co-operation and prosperity' among manufacturers, distributors, and retailers, but not necessarily to the well-being of the customer.

In March 1992, the Fair Trade Commission carried out compulsory inspections of ten Matsushita, Sony, Hitachi, and Toshiba *keiretsu* sales companies suspected of infringing the Anti-Monopoly Law. After a year, the Commission concluded that these companies operated unfair trading practices by proposing 'estimated market prices' which large retailers were 'requested' to adopt. Warnings to stop such practices were issued, but the fact that such a 'request' could be made by the large non-*keiretsu* retailers demonstrates both the tenacity and desperation of the distribution *keiretsu* networks. Before emerging as successful international competitors, Japanese companies had to establish themselves as indigenous concerns. The development of organisational capability in marketing was, like the more well-known instances of improved supply-side and production organisation, an important component of overall competitive achievement. Although the distribution *keiretsu* have played an important role in one stage of Japan's economic development, it appears that they will be forced to change, and that we will see a significant erosion of their influence.

NOTES

1. M. Shimotani, '1930 Nendai "Matsushita Sangyodan" no keisei katei' ('The Process of Formation of the "Matsushita Group" in the 1930s') *Keieishigku* (*Business History*), Vol.21 No.3 (1986).
2. M. Shimotani, 'Corporate Groups and Industrial Fusion', *Kyoto University Economic Review*, Vol.124 (1988). 'Corporate Groups and *Keiretsu* in Japan', *Japanese Yearbook on Business History*, Vol.8 (1992). *Nihon no* keiretsu *to kigyo gurūpu* (*Japan's* Keiretsu *and Corporate Groups*) (Tokyo, 1993).
3. M. Shimotani, 'Senjiki no Matsushita Gurūpu ('The Matsushita Group During the War'), in M. Shimotani and O. Nagashima (eds.), *Senji Nihon keizai no kenkyu* (*Research on the Wartime Japanese Economy*) (Kyoto, 1992).
4. E. Hadley, *Antitrust in Japan* (Princeton, 1970).
5. Shimotani, 'Matsushita no jigyobusei to bunshasei' ('Matsushita's System of Operating Divisions and Spin-offs'), in K. Sakamoto and M. Shimotani (eds.), *Gendai Nihon no kigyo gurūpu* (*Corporate Groups in Modern Japan*) (Tokyo, 1987).
6. Matsushita Electric Industrial, *Matsushita Denki eigyōshi (senzen hen)* (*Marketing History of Matsushita Electric (Prewar Period)*) (1979). Also, K. Ozaki, 'Senzenki Matsushita no channeru kodo to keiei senryaku' ('Matsushita's Prewar Sales Channels and Management Strategy'), *Hikone Ronso* [*Hikone Review*], Vol.257 (1989).
7. Matsushita, *Marketing History (Prewar)*.
8. Ibid.
9. Matsushita Electric Industrial, *Matsushita Denki eigyoshi (senzgo hen)* (*Marketing History of Matsushita Electric (Postwar Period)*) (1980). Also, I.S. Son, 'Kodo seichoki ni okeru kaden ryuutsuu kozo no henka' ('Changes in the Distribution Structure of the Home Appliance and Electronics Industry During the Period of Rapid Economic Growth'), *Keizaigaku kenkyu* [*Economics Research*], Vol.35 (1992).
10. Matsushita, *Marketing History (Postwar)*.
11. Ibid.
12. Matsushita, *Marketing History (Prewar)*.
13. Matsushita, *Marketing History (Postwar)*.

The Rise of the Mass Market and Modern Retailers in Japan

MARIKO TATSUKI

Keisen Jogakuen College
Japan Business History Institute

The nature of the Japanese distributive system has become a source of international contention in recent years. Western nations have argued that its complexities act as barriers to free trade, and have called for its reform. This article examines the history of the distribution system in post-1945 Japan, focusing on the development of the mass market. After a brief introduction, the different types of distributive networks are discussed in part II. Part III presents two case studies on the development of the supermarket in Japan. In part IV, the introduction of American ideas on distribution will be reviewed. Finally, part V will analyse the effects of supermarkets on other distribution systems.

It has been pointed out that the Japanese mass market differs significantly from its American counterpart in three ways. First, the distributive mechanism is complex and long, involving many middlemen between the producer and the consumer. Secondly, the trade relationship at each level of the distributive mechanism is complex and sustained by tight personal and credit connections. And, finally, small family businesses are widespread and their productivity is very low.

These characteristics are in large part due to the history of wholesaling and retailing in the last three centuries. The Japanese distributive system was established in the mid-eighteenth century under the Tokugawa Shogunate, and has remained relatively unchanged ever since.[1] After the Meiji Restoration in 1868, Japanese industrialisation unfolded rapidly, and the Westernisation of people's daily lives began in the large cities. The distributive system which provided these modern commodities to the urban population was established mainly by drapers of silk and cotton kimonos. Large department stores such as Mitsukoshi, Takashimaya, Matsuzakaya and even the relative newcomer Isetan have their roots as kimono retailers of the Edo Period.[2] They had developed their own system of purchasing and trade relationships with suppliers and customers, and adapted them to handle new goods. The wholesalers of cottonwear, who, like their counterparts in silk, have a long history, also transformed themselves after the opening of Japan's ports from handling only domestic goods to dealing in imported goods.

The Japanese distribution system adapted alongside rapid changes in other parts of the economy, notably manufacturing, because the city markets of the Edo era were relatively advanced compared with those of Europe. In Japan, the mass market and popular culture developed during the eighteenth and nineteenth centuries in the large cities of Edo, Kyo (present day Kyoto), and Osaka. The distributive system from western Japan to Edo for all consumer goods including foodstuffs and clothing was established in the early part of the Tokugawa Era, because Edo was a newly established metropolis 600 km away from Kyo and Osaka, the traditional cultural and commercial centres.[3]

The distributive system of the Meiji period and up to the Second World War was built on this tradition, but it began to change after 1945. The Japanese economic system changed dramatically during the Allied Occupation, although the majority of the population were still too poor to be mass consumers. In the course of rapid economic growth in 1955–64, American marketing theory was introduced to Japan, and arguments for distributive innovation emerged.[4] At that time, the inflow of population into urban areas had begun and people's lifestyles were changing with the spread of durable consumer goods such as electric refrigerators, vacuum cleaners, washing machines and televisions. For these new products and for rapidly expanding urban areas, new distributive systems were introduced. On the whole, the speed of change in the distributive system was far slower than the rate of industrial growth, leaving a traditional structure to survive intact (see Table 1). As a result of occupation policies, Japan had a large population with small landholdings. Japanese farmers and retailers could offer a plentiful supply of labour to factories without completely dismantling the small family farm or business. Table 1 shows that, during these years, small family businesses continued to increase in number, although only slowly, and the development of supermarkets did not necessarily lead to the decline of small retailers. Consumers needed high quality service rather than low prices. Housewives shopped daily for fresh food such as vegetables, fish, meat and milk at small neighbourhood retailers,[5] and buying at the nearby retailer was not always expensive. The growth of department stores and supermarkets was supported by various wholesalers. In Japan, modernisation did not mean an abandoning of traditional lifestyles. Consumers required traditional goods as well as westernised ones, and department stores and supermarkets had to keep a wide assortment of articles. Wholesalers also offered various services to retailers, such as price-tag attachment, individual packaging and assortment packs because they could conduct these labour-intensive tasks more efficiently.[6] Small retailers in distant and rural areas needed

TABLE 1
WHOLESALERS AND RETAILERS

	1956	1960	1966	1972
Number of businesses:				
Wholesalers	179,856	225,993	287,208	259,163
Retailers	1,201,273	1,288,292	1,375,394	1,495,510
Department stores	177	292	546	855
Family businesses	972,642	1,024,369	1,060,982	990,945
Ratio of R/W	6.68	5.70	4.79	5.77
Full-Time Shop Clerks:				
Wholesalers	1,293,905	1,928,326	3,041,564	3,007,647
(per outlet)	7.2	8.5	10.6	11.6
Retailers	3,005,173	3,489,293	4,193,421	5,141,377
(per outlet)	2.5	2.3	3.0	3.4
Sales per annum (Yen m):				
Wholesalers	10,728,811	18,468,273	52,082,304	106,780,082
(per shop clerk)	8.29	9.58	17.12	35.50
Retailers	3,010,679	4,315,387	10,683,623	28,292,696
(per shop clerk)	1.0	1.24	2.55	5.50
Ratio of R/W	3.56	4.28	4.87	3.77

1) Ratio of R/W was calculated using the number of shops for the first block, and sales amount for the third block.
2) Family business means private retailer with no full-time employee.
3) Annual sales in 1956 were calculated by the author using estimated sales of family business as 12 times the monthly amount.
4) Statistics on self-service shops including supermarkets began in 1964. The figures are included in 'other retailers'.

Source: MITI, Shogyo Tokei Hyo (Statistics on Commerce for the fiscal year 1956) (Tokyo, 1959), pp.446–47, 450–51; and for the fiscal year 1960 (1963), Business version 1, pp.290 and 312. Tsusan Tokei Kyokai, Sengo no Shogyo Tokei (Statistics in the Post War Period) (Tokyo, 1983), I, pp.364, 440 and 458–59.

a delivery service, and so the number of wholesalers increased even more rapidly than that of retailers (Table 1). Even today, foreign businessmen say that Japanese consumers are the most difficult to please in the world because earning differentials are small and the mass consumer requires high quality and service. People shop almost every day, even though refrigerators are widely owned, because they place emphasis on freshness.[7] They also require individual packaging for clothing and sundries because they dislike even the smallest stains. A complex and small-size distributive system is suited to such a 'mass market', and an American-style system could not cover all of Japan. Nonetheless, supermarkets and discounters developed in the 1960s. They succeeded in making the Japanese market homogeneous in appearance and receptive to a great volume of standardised goods. In the 1970s, supermarkets had satisfied consumer wishes quantitatively, but had to respond qualitative demands. Japanese electric appliance manufacturers and automobile manufacturers made great efforts to cope with this somewhat unique mass market by developing product differentiation within a mass production system, implementing strict quality control and providing an after-sales service; the basic consumer goods makers were pressed even further.

II

POST-WAR INNOVATIONS

Rapid economic growth in Japan returned in 1955. It was assisted by the expansion of a domestic market for durable consumer goods, such as electric refrigerators, washing machines, and televisions. These goods were called 'the Three Sacred Treasures'. Though these household electrical appliances and automobiles were expensive, they became popular and widespread in a short time (See Table 2). The existing distributive network – both wholesale and retail – was too small to deal adequately with these goods. Handling these goods was beyond the capacity of these dealers because they were specialised in their own

TABLE 2
PERCENTAGE OF HOUSEHOLDS OWNING CONSUMER DURABLES, 1967

Annual Income (Yen)	1	2	3	4	5	6	7
Under 300,000	44.6	82.1	0.7	33.8	44.4	16.4	1.1
300 - 599,000	74.9	97.2	4.5	65.3	75.0	33.7	1.2
600 - 899,000	86.4	98.3	10.0	80.6	88.8	54.1	2.5
900 - 1,199,999	87.4	95.0	18.5	87.3	94.0	67.8	3.8
1,200,000 - 1,499,999	92.8	98.5	22.9	93.2	94.1	75.3	5.9
1,500,000 - 1,799,999	94.0	98.4	28.4	93.6	94.6	79.4	7.9
More than 1,799,999	95.7	96.8	40.9	95.1	97.5	88.4	23.6

Notes: 1 = sewing machines; 2 = televisions; 3 = cars; 4 = refrigerators; 5 = washing machines; 6 = vacuum cleaners; 7 = air conditioners.

Source: Keizai Kikakucho, *Shohi to Chochiku no Doko* (*The Trend of Consumption and Savings*), (Tokyo, 1968), pp.114–15.

narrow range of goods, and had insufficient operating funds and limited
floor space. On the other hand, manufacturers were big – both in terms
of manpower and capital – and they had everything they needed to dis-
tribute their products by themselves. During the growth period, labour
migrated from rural areas and new towns developed on the outskirts of
large industrial cities. Supermarkets and discounters began to grow in
these newly emerging suburbs to challenge the big manufacturers. As a
whole, new distributors were still weak and large-scale producers maintained a tight price control over them.

Early innovation in the distribution system can be categorised into
three types: direct distribution by manufacturers; the franchise system;
and the direct sales network. All three are commonly called the distribution *keiretsu*, or hierarchy, with the manufacturer at the top, exercising a
substantial degree of control. These types will be described in detail.

Keiretsu *distribution by manufacturers*

Keiretsu distribution by manufacturers is the most popular of the three
categories. In this system, a manufacturer establishes its own distributive
network, organising existing wholesalers and retailers. Manufacturers
and organised wholesalers jointly establish a wholesale company and
the latter appoints retailers as sole agents. Agents sell at an agreed
price, obtaining rebates and sales promotion assistance from the
manufacturers. *Keiretsu* distribution of this first type has a long history
and is popular among cosmetics retailers and drugstores. These good
are sold in a mass market which grew in a relatively short time. The case
of the largest Japanese cosmetic manufacturer, Shiseido, is illustrative.
The company began to organise retailers as agents in 1924. In 1927, it
established the Shiseido Tokyo Hanbai (Sales) Co. as a wholesaler.
By 1970, there were 72 subsidiary wholesalers all over Japan. Shiseido
agent stores operated a customer association named Hanatsubaki-kai
(the Camellia Club) after the company logo.[8] Shiseido used various
promotional goods and carried out advertising campaigns, utilising its
nationwide sales network. It grew to become the most famous national
brand, with uniform shop design and packaging, and today enjoys a 30
per cent market share.[9] In the 1950s, household electrical appliances
were also sold in this way. Matsushita Electric Industrial Co., famous
for its 'National' and 'Panasonic' brand of electrical goods, such as
batteries and light-bulbs as well as appliances, re-established its sales
network just after the Second World War. It had founded nine branches
and 19 sub-branches all over Japan by 1952, and under them it organised
620 sole agents and 33,000 'national' agents. Matsushita paid rebates,

and, in exchange, agents maintained the agreed prices, which were a trifle lower than those of Matsushita's competitors. At that time. Matsushita sold radios, electric light bulbs and batteries. Though the company was a latecomer to the sale of electric washing machines, transistor radios and other electrical appliances, it advantageously utilised its sales network in addition to active advertising campaigns and consumer-oriented marketing policies. In the late 1950s, the company adopted a full-line merchandise policy, seeking to maintain its nation-wide sole agency network.[10] The distribution system became so firmly established that other Japanese electrical appliance manufacturers such as Hitachi, Toshiba and Mitsubishi, which had their origins in heavy electric machinery, experienced great difficulties in founding their own sales networks.[11]

The Franchise System

The second type of distribution innovation was the franchise system, where control by the manufacturer was stricter than in the first type. A typical case is that of Coca-Cola, which has developed a tight distributive network all over the world. Coca-Cola Japan established a franchise system consisting of 16 bottlers. The company selected them from large Japanese corporations, not existing wholesalers of beverages. For example, Koami Shoten (now the Tokyo Coca-Cola Bottling Co.), which was contracted as the first franchise bottler in Japan in 1952, was the biggest soy sauce distributor in the country. Kinki Coca-Cola was established jointly by Kirin Beer and Shin Mitsubishi Heavy Industries (now Mitsubishi Heavy Industries) in 1960. Contractors received an undiluted solution from Coca-Cola Japan, bottled it and sold it within their sales territories, delivering directly to retailers.[12] Automobiles also relied on the franchise system. Before the Second World War, Ford Japan and GM Japan established dealer networks all over Japan, while Toyota was a newcomer to the market. The Toyota Automatic Loom Works (the forerunner of Toyota Motor Co.) recruited Shotaro Kamiya from GM Japan, and established its own dealer system in 1935. Kamiya had strong objections to the GM dealer system, and wanted to establish an equal partnership between the manufacturer and the dealers. The price of Toyota trucks and cars was set six per cent lower than those of Ford or Chevrolet, even though the price was below the cost of manufacturing. The Law Concerning the Manufacture of Motor Vehicles, which limited the output and virtually prohibited the import of vehicles, was promulgated in 1936, and Toyota Motor and Nissan Motor easily acquired existing dealers of imported cars.

After the war, automobile companies had to reconstruct their factories and could not afford to finance customer instalment plans, despite their being essential to the sale of expensive commodities such as cars. Toyota and Nissan each established an automobile sales company to raise funds for instalment plans, and also undertook active marketing. When distribution under wartime control was dismantled in 1946, Toyota reorganised many of its dealers under its own network and employed the 'GM Standard on Dealer Administration'. Some aspects of the franchise system were adapted to Japanese practice. Territories were large while the number of shops was small in Japan, and manufacturers or sales companies were deeply involved in dealers' finances. As the variety of cars sold increased in the 1960s, Japanese automobile manufacturers introduced the American-type franchise system with small dealers, cash on delivery and open territory. This new system, however, did not fit well with the Japanese market, because dealers and consumers were short of cash and strong financial support was necessary. As a result, the relationship between manufacturers and dealers is a close one in Japan even under the franchise system; so it can be considered a form of the *keiretsu* system.[13]

The Japanese-style dealer system also works as a post-sale service network, and the larger franchises have their own service stations. In the case of Honda Motors, which was a latecomer in the car market, dealers were too small and the company had to close the gap by establishing its own direct sales outlets and service network. The quality of the service network is a very important consideration for Japanese consumers when choosing a car.

The Direct Sales Network

Some manufacturers established direct sales networks. In the case of sewing machines, distribution systems were created before the Second World War through the introduction of a sole agency system similar to ones for other household appliances. After the war, more than 50 manufacturers were competing against each other, and, in order to survive, manufacturers began to introduce the direct sales system. Brother Sewing Machine, the biggest domestic machine manufacturer, decided to invest in its own sales network in 1949, a little later than its competitors, such as Singer Sewing Machine. The Tokyo Brother Sewing Machine Sales Co., which initially fell behind its competitors in market share, changed its marketing policy, vigorously establishing sales outlets in 1966, and acquiring the largest share of the market in the Tokyo district within three years. The company changed its policy because the agent system could not respond quickly and appropriately to consumers' needs.[14] Besides sewing machine manufacturers, a well-known bed manufacturer, France Bed, also adopted a direct sales policy. In this case, beds were ill-suited to the Japanese lifestyle and the company had to advertise vigorously. But, in general, the direct sales system is not popular in Japan because it requires a big outlay of capital if a nationwide network is to be created.

III

THE IMPACT OF SUPERMARKETS

In 1957, the 'House-wives' Store, Daiei, opened, proclaiming the dawn of the supermarket in Japan (see Table 3). Daiei was ranked tenth in sales among Japanese retailers in 1963, fifth in 1968 and first in 1972. The 1960s was a decade of growth for Daiei and for many other supermarkets. From the figures in Table 4, one can see that they became equivalent in size to department stores. The 1960s also brought a shortage of young labour and rising labour costs. The supermarkets dealt with this problem through mass sales and low prices, purchasing in large quantities and rationalising the distribution and sales system. The Japanese supermarket was unique in selling groceries, clothing and household commodities including home appliances. While the United States experienced two distributive revolutions – one in the 1930s and another in the 1950s[15] – Japan underwent the transformation in the

TABLE 3
SELF-SERVICE SHOPS, 1964–72

	Number	%	Space 1000 sqm	Clerks No.	%	Sales Yen m	%
1964	3,620	0.3	1342	89,429	2.4	39,2373	4.7
1966	4,790	0.4	1557	105,083	2.5	581,145	5.4
1968	7,062	0.5	2780	142,896	3.1	1,028,570	6.2
1970	9,403	0.6	4188	173,072	3.5	1,612,459	7.4
1972	10,634	0.7	5587	207,119	4.0	2,447,583	8.7

Notes: 1) Percentage shares indicate the ratio with the total of all retailers.
2) Self-service shops include retailing corporations with more than 100 sq.m. of shop space and where more than 50 per cent of the space is used for self-service retailing.

Source: *Sengo no Shogyo Tokei*, pp.458–60.

TABLE 4
SALES RANKING OF RETAILERS (1972)

Name	Type	Head Office	Sales Ybn	Outlets	Yen bn per Outlet
Daiei	supermarkets	Osaka	305.2	90	3.39
Mitsukoshi	depart. stores	Tokyo	292.4	12	24.37
Daimaru	depart. stores	Osaka	213.1	6	35.52
Takashima-ya	depart. stores	Tokyo	199.4	4	49.85
Seiyu Stores	supermarkets	Tokyo	166.8	96	1.81
Seibu Depart. Stores	depart. stores	Tokyo	155.0	10	15.50
JUSCO	supermarkets	Osaka	155.0	131	1.16
Matsuzaka-ya	depart. stores	Nagoya	149.3	6	24.88
Nichii	supermarkets	Osaka	144.2	156	0.92
Uni	supermarkets	Nagoya	126.4	108	1.17
Marui	monthly installment chain store	Tokyo	95.2	30	3.17
Daiichikaden	(household electricals)	Tokyo	18.1	70	0.25
Kiosk	various	Tokyo	161.4	?	?

Source: Nikkei Ryutsu Shimbun, *Ranking Ryutsu Kakumei* (*Ranking of Retailers*) (Tokyo, 1987), and Tokyo Keizai Shinpo, *Kaisha Shikiho* (*Quarterly Report of Corporations*) (Tokyo, 1970)

1960s alone. Usually, Japanese supermarkets call themselves *ryohan-ten* (mass retailers) due to this unique characteristic of being supermarkets and discounters at the same time. The process of growth occurred through trial and error and competition against the established distribution system. To demonstrate this, we will examine the cases of two nationwide supermarkets; one is Daiei, the largest and originally based in the Kansai area (an area in western Japan centred around Osaka), and the other is Seiyu, the second largest until the 1980s and now the third largest, and originally based in the Kanto area centred around Tokyo.

Daiei started as a pharmacy in Osaka in 1957. Though small, it sold every item at a dramatically lower price than rivals, usually at a discount rate of over 30 per cent. In the post-Korean War recession, the company took advantage of the large inventories held by pharmaceutical manufacturers. The great success of Daiei was soon followed by a nearby competitor, Higuchi Pharmacy, now one of Japan's largest drug chain stores. Isao Nakauchi, the founder of Daiei, was inventive enough to move 'from drugs into candies and other foods and from cosmetics and toiletries into hardware'. He also continued to build his pharmaceutical chain store, opening a second outlet the next year.[16] It was the dawn of Japanese supermarkets. Daiei purchased drugs from wholesalers and sold them at prices 30 to 40 per cent lower than the manufacturers' official prices.[17] The existing pharmacies protested to the wholesalers and manufacturers, saying that the Daiei price was even lower than their purchase price. Every time Daiei constructed a new store, the local pharmacy association opposed it. The pharmaceutical manufacturers took measures to cut supplies, but their attempts to impose restrictive practices were not successful. Difficulties between pharmacy associations and Daiei finally led to restrictive government action, despite the company having the support of consumers. In 1963, when Daiei had eight stores, the Drugs, Cosmetics and Medical Instruments Act was revised, and the opening of new pharmacies within a given distance from existing ones was prohibited. Daiei struggled against pharmacy associations, manufacturers and legislation, but in the end succeeded in its objectives. In 1975, the Act was revised by the Superior Court.[18]

Daiei concentrated on buying first-class products in the 1960s. In the case of Ajinomoto, a maker of synthetic seasoning and processed foodstuffs, Daiei had a special buying route, about which wholesalers and retailers complained. The company used the Jinmi Corporation, one of Ajinomoto's major wholesalers. Its president, Saburosuke Suzuki, suggested to the chairman of Ajinomoto that he should go and see a Daiei store where his lines sold well. As a result, he instructed the manager of his Osaka branch to sell directly to Daiei. Daimaru, the biggest department store in Osaka, protested in 1962, saying that it would not deal with the Ajinomoto Co. if it sold Ajinomoto gift sets of foodstuffs to Daiei at a discount. It was compelled to withdraw because the Ajinomoto gift set was a very popular item during the gift season. The Ajinomoto case was an exception. In other cases, Daiei had to fight vigorously against the manufacturers' market control. It stocked up on merchandise before beginning a fight, and continued discounting until the manufacturer proposed a compromise. Using these methods Daiei succeeded in obtaining many concessions, including Morinaga baby formula, Nisshin Shokuhin instant noodles, Yukijirushi butter, Nestle instant coffee, and Unilever margarine.[19] Daiei completed the organisational structure of its chain store operation in 1962. Isao Nakauchi attended the meeting of the Association of Supermarkets in the United States and learnt American marketing and merchandising methods. In 1963, the head office of the company was remodelled to house the merchandising department, which was established in the previous year as an independent organisation from the sales department. It also acted as a distribution centre, a computer centre and a meat processing and packing centre. The first store-brand sports shirt was developed in the same year in association with Toyobo, the largest cotton mill and clothing manufacturer in Japan. In 1963, the company moved to become a national chain store, establishing Fukuoka Daiei in the Kyushu area, merging with a small supermarket in Tokyo in 1964, funding Shikoku Daiei, and creating a store in Okayama. Outlets numbered 20 in 1964.[20]

Seibu Stores was established slightly earlier than Daiei. Its three stores were incorporated in 1956 following the reorganisation of Seibu Department Stores. It had neither a chain store policy nor a location strategy and administered a number of small, poorly performing stores. The company put into practice new management techniques in its Takatanobaba store in Tokyo in 1962. The outlet introduced a self-service system, equipping checkout counters with cash registers. It followed the lead of Daiei, which had introduced a central checkout system in 1959. They called it 'SSDDS', which meant self service discount department store. Seibu learnt of this system in the United States, when the National Cash Resister Co. held a Seminar on Modern Merchandising Methods, inviting retailers all over the world in order to demonstrate the American distributive system and marketing and management methods. Seibu Department Store staff attended the seminar, and the reorganisation of the Takatanobaba store followed. They tried to devise a packaging method for every item, from eggs and soy bean paste to underwear and socks. It took until 1965 for the store to take on the appearance of a supermarket, with every item packed and displayed on the shelf. Rationalisation proceeded concurrently, and the number of shop clerks at the Takatanobaba store decreased from 175 in 1962 to 78 in 1963 and to 55 in 1964. After this success, Seibu proceeded to introduce the same methods in other stores. At the Hibarigaoka store, which is located in a large housing complex, the trial lasted only several months, as sales decreased and customers went to competitors. Takatanobaba is located near Shinjuku and there were no other supermarkets nearby. It was clear that Japanese consumers preferred personal sales, because the self-service system was still imperfect. Seibu sent clerks to Daiei and Itoyokado to observe their operations. While Seibu learned about US administrative methods such as central purchasing and control systems, it failed to adapt them to its actual operations.

Seibu Stores changed its name to Seiyu Stores in 1963. The company established seven outlets in 1964 and three to four stores in each of the following years, seeking the scale economies of a chain operation. Seiyu reviewed its merchandising policy, which was largely based on the product selection of a department store, and implemented a new approach in 1968. The company began to standardise its merchandise; it developed a new price strategy; it began to encourage central purchasing and planning; a distribution system, combining direct delivery by wholesalers and central delivery control, was refined; and new merchandise, including own-brand labels, was introduced. Seiyu's development occurred without the disputes faced by Daiei. Its weakness was its origin as a department store. The company could easily buy big manufacturers' goods but its retail prices were expensive compared to other supermarkets, especially Daiei, which pursued low prices at every opportunity. On the other hand, Seiyu had an advantage in household appliances such as televisions, washing machines and refrigerators. In the early 1960s, electric appliance manufacturers which followed Matsushita and Sharp into the household market had unsatisfactory sales networks. Seiyu sold their products aggressively and succeeded in increasing the variety of merchandise and the discount rate at the same time.[21]

IV

THE LESSONS OF AMERICAN RETAILING

American merchandising theory has greatly influenced the development of supermarkets in Japan. Shuji Hayashi, a business economist, studied the American mass market and published a book entitled *Ryutsu Kakumei* in 1962.[22] He predicted the development of supermarkets and the decline of small retailers, as well as a fall in the number of wholesalers, and he advocated the construction of a modern mass distributive system which linked mass production and mass consumption. The book popularised the idea of a distributive revolution and interested both distributors and the general public. Hajime Sato, who worked for National Cash Register (NCR), was eager to introduce an American distributive revolution.[23] He criticised Hayashi and, referring to empirical studies, argued that Hayashi's argument was too simple and neglectful of the interests of the consumer. Hayashi did not understand the real American distributive system in which retailers were large enough to bargain against big manufacturers and establish quality testing facilities. Sato warned that Hayashi's ideas might lend support to control by large producers rather than price competition by retailers.[24] Sato also invited Japanese participants to attend the Modern Merchandising Method (MMM) Seminar held at the head office of NCR in Ohio. Seiyu Stores and the Takashimaya Shopping Centre were a direct result of his activities.[25]

Isao Nakauchi flew to Chicago in 1962 to attend the 25th International Supermarkets Conference as the representative of Japan. He was deeply influenced by the message of J.F. Kennedy, who declared the consumers' doctrine and the slogan of the Conference to be 'Mobility, Courage, New Ideas, Integration'. He was convinced of the future role of supermarkets and sought to introduce change. The *35 Year History of Daiei* locates this event as the real start of Daiei as a supermarket; and, after his return, Daiei began to construct a distribution centre and established a merchandising department. Shun'ichi Atsumi, a participant in the MMM Seminar, founded the Retailing Centre upon his return and assumed the task of teaching American chain store operation theory to retailers. Ito-Yokado, Seiyu, Benimaru and many other supermarkets attended the sessions held at the Centre and put the theory into practice. Atsumi's approach was a simple interpretation of American theory, consisting of central purchasing and the standardisation of shops and merchandise. It was based on 'shop-worker' theory, in which merchandisers are the brain and shops engage only in day-to-day work. The system, however, was later revised when Seiyuwhen store managers rose in revolt against merchandisers. But Atsumi's chain operations and techniques generally succeeded. In 1964, many of the supermarkets which grew rapidly without the American approach went bankrupt. The 175 which folded were followed by 191 in the next year, when the total number of supermarkets in operation was about 700.[26] On the other hand, the number of large corporations to be found among supermarkets grew steadily. A survey by *Nihon Keizai Shinbun* (*Japan Economic News*) in 1967 revealed that 40 per cent of the retailers with more than four billion yen in annual sales were supermarkets. The supermarkets, however, held a share of the market far smaller than ten per cent of all retail business in the 1960s. They could trade in the mass market with simple techniques of chain operation, which they had developed without facing the complexities of other parts of the Japanese market whose needs could be fulfilled by small retailers.

V

THE LESSONS FOR JAPANESE RETAILING

In the late 1950s and 1960s, supermarkets expanded rapidly. The retail sale price maintenance policy of big manufacturers, implemented through the *keiretsu* sales network, was established in the beginning of this period. It is doubtful, however, whether these sales networks offered merchandise at acceptable prices, and, in the mid-1960s, discount stores developed to fill a market niche. For example, Akihabara, the area of electrical appliance and camera discounters in Tokyo, evolved in these years. Some supermarkets originated from discount stores, because in order to grow they had to extend their fight against the established distribution system. One effective method of strengthening their sales power was to sell foodstuffs which attracted the daily grocery shoppers to their stores. Unlike the US, there was no grocery chain store in Japan at that time, and the food floors of department stores were popular. The newly developing supermarkets became a closer and more convenient alternative to the department stores, which were usually located at commuter train terminal stations. Daiei is a typical example. Ito-Yokado, Futagi and Shiro, forerunners of JUSCO and Nichii have the same origin. Because of its department store background, Seiyu outlets looked like small department stores and, in food, clothing and household articles, it struggled to maintain low prices. Other super-markets with a department store origin, such as Tobu Stores, also designed its shops like miniatures of the parent company and were equally uncompetitive in price.

Nakauchi, the founder of Daiei, defined himself as 'a destroyer of price' and said in his memoirs that 'The history of Daiei is a history of fighting. We challenged ourselves and trained ourselves through fights against manufacturers and distributors'.[27] The company battled not only against the pharmacy associations but also against meat packers and vegetable dealers. Only after it had grown to a certain size did it take on the big manufacturers. In 1965, Daiei's sales exceeded 30 billion yen, and large-scale producers could no longer ignore it. Moreover, by this time, the Japanese economy was in a severe depression after ten years of high growth, and the big manufacturers were eager to maintain resale prices. Kao Corporation, the largest maker of soap, detergent and toiletries, stopped supplying goods to Daiei in response to its discounting. Daiei took Kao to court on its resale price maintenance policy. It is well known that Daiei challenged Matsushita on its price controls and won. Again in 1965, Matsushita took strong measures to maintain its policy and strengthen its *keiretsu* network. In order to stop the supply of 'National' brand products to Daiei, Matsushita tried to track down Daiei's purchasing route by tracing its products coded with hidden numbers and by watching the numbers of trucks delivering goods to Daiei's distribution centre. It also bought up all of its products at Daiei stores. The retailer responded by offering evidence of Matsushita's resale price policy to the Fair Trade Commission. In 1967, the Commission inspected Matsushita and recommended reform. Though the judgment took a long time, the incident had a positive effect on the Japanese consumers' movement, then in its infancy. Matsushita and other electric appliances manufacturers were forced to change their attitudes and Daiei was able to purchase household electric appliances with ease.[28] Nevertheless, consumers did criticise supermarkets for failing to offer low prices at all times. Small retailers could compete with supermarkets by taking advantage of low labour costs and using unpaid family members. Most supermarkets did not rationalise their production and distribution systems. Kiyonari Tadao, a business economist, stated, 'in the mid-1960s supermarkets were established as big firms and began to enlarge their business rapidly, making it difficult to buy at a low price and take competitive advantage of small manufacturers and monopolistic interests'.[29]

Japan's gross national product per capita exceeded US $1,000 in current prices in 1966, while it had been about $300 in 1950. The lifestyle of the Japanese people had changed greatly in the decade of rapid economic growth since 1955, and westernised consumer goods became popular, keeping pace with the increase in income and the building of city apartments. In the 1960s, central areas of large cities such as Tokyo and Osaka expanded, and many residential complexes and suburban housing projects were constructed. The rapid growth of the supermarket was accelerated by its ability to supplement existing distributive networks, not replace them. The number of supermarkets increased most rapidly in these new residential areas. Ito-Yokado, which started its chain operations in the Kanto district in 1960, pursued a strategy of constructing larger stores in suburban areas easily accessible by car, in anticipation of motorisation. Seiyu established shops in front of suburban train stations along commuter railways such as the Seibu Railways, the Chuo Line and the Sobu Line of Japan Railways and Tokyu Railways. The growth of supermarkets did not trespass on the business of existing small retailers; both large retailers and small family retailers grew hand in hand, though the speed of growth for large retailers was much faster than that of their smaller counterparts. Supermarkets tried to establish their superiority over small retailers, although the purchasing of goods in large volume and mass marketing did not

TABLE 5
THE SCALE OF RETAILERS

	Space per Shop sq.m.	Employees per Shop	Sales per Shop 1000 Yen	No. of Shops
All Retailers:				
1964	29.9	2.92	6,390	1,304,536
1968	34.2	3.07	9,980	1,432,436
1972	43.2	3.21	16,210	1,494,643
Self-Service Shops:				
1964	371	24.70	108,390	3,624
1968	394	20.23	145,650	7,062
1972	525	19.48	230,170	10,634
Department Stores:				
1964	10,361	602	4,346,440	-
1968	11,049	568	5,753,840	236
1972	12,897	553	9,179,800	282
Family Stores:				
1964	20.2	1.81	2,380	1,035,433
1968	21.9	1.86	3,540	1,075,270
1972	23.0	1.89	4,350	990,047

Source: Wagakuni no Shogyo, 1973, pp.34–35.

necessarily result in this desired goal.[30] With the exception of Daiei, they had no distribution centres until the late 1960s, and they depended on wholesalers for most of the distributive functions. The low price was primarily a result of low profits[31] and the low wages of store clerks and wholesale workers.[32] Above all, the scale of supermarkets was still too small in comparison to department stores (see Table 5) for them to have any bargaining power against big manufacturers and wholesalers. In the early 1970s, they were still acquiring the necessary size. On the other hand, small family retailers grew in number at the rate of two to three per cent a year, although this figure was far smaller than the rate of Japanese economic growth. It is clear that, at that time, many people chose the convenience and good service of these small shops, and supermarkets could not hold a dominant position. But, in the mid-1970s, they finally began to mature into a new force in the distribution system.[33]

NOTES

1. Publications generally argue that the major cause of these differences is that there was no mass market before the Second World War in Japan and that the mass market began to develop in the first period of high economic growth after 1955, when new distributive systems were introduced into Japan. See Yotaro Yoshino, *Nihon no Marketing: Tekio to Kakushin* (*Japanese Marketing: Adaptation and Innovation*) (Tokyo, 1976), pp.47–100; T. Kiyonari, *Nihon Ryutsu Sanngyo no Kakushin* (*The Innovation of Japan's Distributors*) (Tokyo, 1975), pp.45–50.

2. Refer to company histories of each department store; additionally, see *The International Directory of Company Histories*, Vol.5 (London, 1993). On Echigoya, the forerunner of Mitsukoshi, see J. Roberts, *Mitsui: Three Centuries of Japanese Business* (New York, 1973). pp.13–22.

3. A, Hayami, *Nihon Keizai-shi I: Keizai Shakai no Seiritsu* (*Japanese Economic History I: The Establishment of Economic Society*) (Tokyo, 1988), pp.218–58.

4. The most popular reformer was Shuji Hayashi. Refer to his *Ryutsu Kakumei* (*Distributive Revolution*) (Tokyo, 1962). He was criticised in 1971 by Hajime Sato, *Ryutsu Sangyo Kakumei* (*Revolution by the Distributing Industries*) (Tokyo, 1971), pp.7–12.

5. At that time, in the traditional residential districts in Tokyo, vegetable and fish retailers went door-to-door for orders every day, and milk and tofu (soy-bean cake) were delivered every morning. Such convenient service had been traditional since the Edo period, and it was regarded as indispensable to city life.

6. In general, the wage level was higher in large corporations in the 1950s and 1960s. See Takafusa Nakamura and Konosuke Odaka, *Nihon Keizai-shi 6: Niju Kozo* (*Japanese Economic History 6: Dual Structure*) (Tokyo, 1989).

7. For a housewife to go shopping every day, the density and number of retailers had to be high. The number of hardware stores, kitchenware and liquor shops increased until 1960, rice shops until 1954, and dairy shops, butchers, fish mongers and fiower shops were still increasing in number in the 1980s. See Tsusan Tokei Kyokai, *Sengo no Shogyo Tokei Hyo* (*Commercial Statistics In the Post War Years*), Vol.1 (Tokyo, 1983).

8. See *Shiseido Hyakunen-shi* (*Centenary History of Shiseido*) (Tokyo, 1972); *Shiseido Hanbai Kaisha 50nen-shi* (*Fifty Years History of Shiseido Sales Co.*) (Tokyo, 1978); *Shiseido Senden Shi* (*The History of Shiseido Advertisements*) Vols.1–3 (Tokyo, 1979).

9. One can easily find similar cases in cosmetic, food, and drug companies. Examples include the Kao Corporation, a chemical company which started as a soap manufacturer. See *Kao-shi Hyakunen* (*The Centennial History of Kao Corporation*) (Tokyo, 1993); Ajinomoto Co., a food processing company and the world's first and largest producer of monosodium glutamate. See *Ajinomoto Shashi* (*The Company History of Ajinomoto*), Vols.1–2 (Tokyo, 1971 and 1972); and Takeda Pharmaceutical Industries, Japan's largest pharmaceutical company. See *Takeda 200 Nenshi* (*A Bicentenal History of Takeda*) (Osaka, 1983).

10. See *Matsushita Denki 50nen no Ryakushi* (*50 Years History of Matsushita*), (Osaka, 1968); K. Noda *Matsushita Konosuke: Sono Hito to Jigyo* (*Konosuke Matsushita: Personality and Business*) (Tokyo, 1967); Y. Okamoto *Hitachi to Matsushita* (*Hitachi and Matsushita*) (Tokyo, 1979).

11. See *Hitachi Seisakujo Shi*, Vols.1–3, (Tokyo, 1949, 1960, 1971); Mitsubishi Electric, *Kengyo Kaiko* (*Retrospective on the Foundation*) (Tokyo, 1951); *Toshiba 100 Nenshi* (*Centenary History of Toshiba*) (Tokyo, 1977); T. Okamoto, *Waga Kuni Kaden Sangyo ni okeru Kigyo Kodo* (*Business Behaviour in the Japanese Household Electric Appliances Industry*) (Tokyo, 1973).

12. See Coca-Cola (Japan) Corporation, *Aisarete 30 Nen* (*Loved for 30 Years*) (Tokyo, 1987); Tokyo Coca-Cola Bottling, *Sawayaka 25 Nen* (*Fresh for 25 Years*) (Tokyo, 1982); Kinki Coca-Cola, *30 Nen no Ayumi* (*30 Years' History*) (Tokyo, 1991).

13. See *Sozo Kagirinaku: Toyota Jidosha 50 Nennshi* (*50 Years' History of Toyota Motor*

Co.) (Tokyo, 1987); *Motarizeshon to tomoni* (*History of Toyota Motor Sales Co.*) (Tokyo, 1970); *Tokyo Toyota Jidosha 40 Nenshi* (*40 Years' History of Tokyo Toyota Motor Sales*) (Tokyo, 1986); *Tokyo Toyopetto 30 Nennshi* (*30 Years' History of Tokyo Toyopet*) (Tokyo, 1983); *Nissan Jidosha 30 Nennshi* (*30 Years' History of Nissan Motor Co.*) (Tokyo, 1965); *Honda no Ayumi* (*A History of Honda Motor Co.*) (Tokyo, 1985). In English, see Toyota Motor Co., *Toyota: A History of the First 50 Years* (Tokyo, 1987).

14. See *Brother no Ayumi* (*A History of Brother Company*) (Tokyo, 1971).
15. Yoshiro Miwa *et al.*, *Nihon no Ryutsu* (*Japanese Distribution*) (Tokyo, 1989). See also T. McCraw, *America Versus Japan* (Boston, 1990), Figure 3–3, p.107. This chart was originally prepared by the Retailing Centre and was widely circulated in Japanese retailing circles.
16. Nakauchi, *Waga Yasuuri Tetsugaku* (*My Philosophy as a Discounter*) (Tokyo, 1969).
17. Manufacturers' official prices were approved in 1953 as an exception to the Anti-Monopoly Law.
18. See *For the Customers: Daiei Group 35 Nen no Kiroku* (*A 35 Years' Record of Daiei*), (Osaka, 1992).
19. See *Ajinomoto Shashi*.
20. See Daiei, *35 Years' History*, and Nakauchi, *Waga Yasuuri Tetsugaku*.
21. See T. Yui *et al.*, *Sezon no Rekishi* (*A History of Saison Group*) (Tokyo, 1991), Ch.3, Sections 1 and 4.
22. S. Hayashi, *Ryutsu Kakumei*.
23. See U. Kitazato, *Hanbai Kakumei ni Yureru Amerika: Discount Store no Shutsugen* (*America in the Midst of a Sales Revolution: The Coming of Discount Stores*) (Tokyo), *Economist*, Aug. 1962. U. Kitazato is the pen name of H. Sato.
24. H. Sato, *Ryutsu Sangyo Kakumei*, pp.7–9 and *Nihon no Ryutsu Kiko* (*Distributive System In Japan*) (Tokyo, 1974).
25. *A History of Saison*, pp.383–4; *Takashima-ya 150 Nenshi* (*150 Years' History of Takashima-ya*) (Tokyo, 1982), pp.148–52, 215–16.
26. *Asahi Nenkan 1966* (*Asahi Yearbook*), p.439. The number of bankruptcies is available in a survey from the Tokyo Shogyo Koshinjo (Tokyo Credit Bureau). The number of supermarkets is in Ministry of International Trade and Commerce, *Supamaketto ni Kannsuru Chosa* (*A Survey on Supermarkets*) (1965).
27. Nakauchi, *Waga Yasuuri*. In those days, even Daiei was limited in its bargaining power and was not always a price setter. Retailers could not determine a product's cost because private brand merchandise was not then popular.
28. Daiei, *35 Years History*. Daiei fought against the electrical appliances manufacturers again in 1970. The company developed a low price colour television with Crown Electric and sold it 30 to 40 thousand yen cheaper than other televisions. This development followed a speech of the chairman of the Fair Trade Commission that the electrical appliances manufacturers were guilty of dual pricing. The Daiei television proved tremendously popular, but Crown faced pressures from large parts manufacturers.
29. T. Kiyonari, 'Taishu Shohi Shakai to Ryutsu Kakumei' ('Mass Markets and the Distributive Revolution'), p.77, in T. Iida, T. Kiyonari, *et al.*, *Gendai Nihon Keizaishi* (*Modern Japanese Economic History*) (Tokyo, 1976).
30. The financial condition of Seiyu was rather strained, because of the rapid increase in the number of stores. See Sueaki Takaoka, *Seiyu Store no Ryutsu Shihai Senryaku* (*The Strategy of Seiyu Stores for Controlling Distribution*) (Tokyo, 1970); *Sezon no Rekishi*, pp.432–4. Not just Seiyu, but most supermarkets were not in a favourable financial condition, because of their massive investments, mostly in land and shops, financed by loans from banks and other financial institutions.
31. In 1973, the ratio of profit to sales for supermarkets was lower than that of department stores. Ito-Yokado recorded the highest profit ratio among supermarkets, at only 2.0 per cent; Daiei's ratio was 1.1 per cent; and Seiyu was 0.65 per cent. The comparison, however, is not entirely accurate because accounting systems differ

88 THE ORIGINS OF JAPANESE INDUSTRIAL POWER

somewhat between supermarkets and department stores. See Ministry of International Trade and Industry, *Wagakuni no Shogyo* (*Statistics on Commerce*) (Tokyo, 1973).

32. There are no statistics on the wage levels of wholesalers, but wholesalers are small businesses and it is widely pointed out that a dual wage structure existed until the 1980s between large corporations on one hand and small and medium enterprises on the other. See also note 6.

33. In 1973, the Diet passed the Large Scale Retail Store Act, which served as a restrictive regulation over supermarkets. As a result, Japanese small retailers could prolong their lives for 20 years. Small-size chain stores called 'convenience stores' developed after the establishment and the success of Seven-Eleven Japan Inc. in 1974. Many supermarkets including Daiei and Seiyu also opened similar outlets. The Act was reviewed in 1990 to make the establishment of large stores easier and a change in the retailing industry is now expected. See T.K. McCraw and P.A. O'Brien, 'Production and Distribution: Competition Policy and Industry Structure', in T. McCraw (ed.), *America Versus Japan*, on the relationship between the Act and the industry.

The Evolution of the Financial System in Post-War Japan

TETSUJI OKAZAKI
University of Tokyo

Many scholars, businessmen and policy makers regard the Japanese experience as a model for developing countries, while others try to derive lessons for the transforming socialist countries of eastern Europe. The Japanese financial system in the post-war period has been of particular interest, and recent research has focused on the roles of the main banks that support industrial enterprises[1] and complementary institutional arrangements.[2] The main banks were supported by the regulatory framework created by the Ministry of Finance (MOF), public financial institutions such as the Japan Development Bank (JDB), as well as the industrial policies of the Ministry of International Trade and Industry (MITI). The relationships and functions of these institutions have never been fully investigated and documented, and this paper will focus on their historical evolution and inter-relating roles, as well as exploring the main bank system.

II

JAPANESE FINANCIAL STRUCTURE

The sectoral saving–investment balance of post-war Japan was generally characterised by a large deficit in the corporate sector, a large surplus in the personal sector, and a small surplus in the public sector (Table 1). A major aim of the financial system was, as is well known, to intermediate the flow of funds from the personal to the corporate sector.[3] The process of financial intermediation had distinct characteristics, and these are outlined in *The Flow of Funds Accounts*, published by the Bank of Japan. The personal sector overwhelmingly preferred cash and deposits as safe and divisible assets, and the ratio of bonds and stocks was very low (Table 2). The assets of households being small on average, the risks and transaction costs of bonds and stocks were too great a disincentive. During the Second World War, the Japanese economy lost about a quarter of its national assets, and the personal sector was badly affected. The rich, who had bought bonds and stocks in the pre-war period,

TABLE 1

SAVING-INVESTMENT BALANCE BY SECTOR 1955–74

	% of GNP		
	Corporate	Household	Government
1955-59	-8.9	7.7	0.5
1960-64	-10.9	8.2	1.4
1965-69	-7.7	6.8	0.7
1970-74	-10.9	10.1	0.6

Source: Economic Planning Agency (ed.), *Choki Sokyu Suikei Kokumin Keizai Keisan Hokoku* (*Long-Term Retroactive Estimation of National Accounts*).

TABLE 2

APPLICATION OF FUNDS BY PERSONAL SECTOR (%), 1955–74

	1955-59	1960-64	1965-69	1970-74
Total	100.0	100.0	100.0	100.0
Currency	4.4	5.7	6.3	6.8
Deposits	61.4	53.7	59.0	65.3
Trusts	4.1	5.2	6.5	6.3
Insurance	11.9	9.6	13.0	13.0
Government Bonds	0.2	-0.1	{	0.7
Public Corp. Bonds	0.3	1.0	{ 7.1	1.3
Bank Debentures	2.1	2.6	{	3.7
Industrial Bonds	0.4	0.4	{	1.0
Stocks & Securities				
Investment Trusts	9.2	11.0	2.1	1.3
Other	6.0	10.9	6.0	0.6

Source: Bank of Japan, *Flow of Funds Accounts*.

suffered the majority of losses as a result of post-war reforms and hyper-inflation.[4] Most of the funds acquired by the financial sector were made available as loans (Table 3). In other words, the ratio of bonds and stocks compared to total assets to be found in the financial sector was low in post-war Japan.

There was a range of institutions within the financial sector. The commercial banks held the largest share of funds. They gathered deposits from both the corporate and the personal sectors and invested

TABLE 3
APPLICATION OF FUNDS BY THE FINANCIAL SECTOR (%), 1955–1974

	1955-59	1960-64	1965-69	1970-74
Total	100.0	100.0	100.0	100.0
Currency & Deposits	2.0	1.7	1.2	2.4
Government Bonds	1.1	0.9	{	3.2
Public Corp. Bonds	2.0	1.7	{ 14.5	2.2
Bank Debentures	3.8	2.9	{	3.1
Industrial Bonds	3.9	3.2	{	1.4
Stocks & Securities				
Investment Trusts	6.4	6.8	2.5	3.8
Call Money	0.7	0.1	-0.3	0.8
Loans	77.5	77.6	79.0	78.5
Other	2.6	5.1	3.1	4.5

Source: Bank of Japan, *Flow of Funds Accounts.*

them in loans or securities. There were moreover two types of commercial bank. The city banks included Mitsui, Mitsubishi, Sumitomo, Fuji, Daiichi (Kangyo), and Sanwa, and they have been defined as having 'their headquarters in a metropolitan area and nationwide networks of many banking branches'. The regional banks had 'their headquarters in large or medium-sized cities throughout the country and carry on most of their business in the prefecture in which the head office is located'.[5] There were three long-term credit banks: the Industrial Bank of Japan (reorganised in 1952), the Long-Term Credit Bank of Japan (established in 1952), and the Nippon Credit Bank (established in 1957). The purpose of these credit banks was to supply long-term loans to industries which were particularly capital-intensive, and they were consequently permitted to issue bank debentures as a means of raising the necessary funds.[6] Besides city banks and long-term credit banks there were trust banks specialised foreign exchange banks, insurance companies, and institutions for small firms, agriculture, forestry and fishery. In the public sector, some institutions such as the Japan Development Bank and the Export-Import Bank of Japan engaged in policy-based finance.[7] Looking at the corporate sector, we find that most of the funds were raised from these financial institutions, especially the commercial banks (Table 4). This pattern can be discerned in the flow of funds to industry for the purchase of equipment (Table 5). Nevertheless, the links between specific industries and financial institutions did differ. Some, notably electricity, shipping, and coalmining, depended heavily on

TABLE 4
FUNDS TO INDUSTRY (%), 1955–1974

	1955-59	1960-64	1965-69	1970-74
Total	100.0	100.0	100.0	100.0
Stock	13.5	16.2	6.2	5.8
Industrial Bonds	4.4	4.5	3.3	3.1
Loans	82.1	79.4	90.5	91.1
Private Financial Institutions	73.3	72.8	81.2	83.1
Long-Term Financial Institutions	6.2	5.1	6.1	6.5
Public Financial Institutions	6.7	5.2	8.0	7.1
Other	2.1	1.4	1.3	0.9

Source: Toyo Keizai Shinposha, *Showa Kokusei Soran*, Vol.2 (Tokyo, 1991).

public finance, the JDB being the main contributor. There was also a heavy reliance on bonds issues by electricity, iron and steel, and transportation concerns. Variations were reflective of the historical circumstances that influenced institutional arrangements and the policies of government.

III

CITY BANKS, THE REGULATORY FRAMEWORK, AND
INDUSTRIAL POLICY

As previously mentioned, a number of economists have come to regard the main banks as the most remarkable characteristic of the post-war Japanese financial structure. Aoki *et al.*, in one of the most important recent contributions to the literature, define the main bank arrangements as 'an informal set of practices, institutional arrangements, and behaviour patterns that constitute a system of corporate financing and governance',[8] and this definition is adopted here. Links include reciprocal shareholdings, the appointment of directors, loans and credits, bond-issue trusteeships, payment settlements, and the provision of foreign exchange. These functions stem from the main bank's ability to monitor the performance and activities of client firms, although they are additionally contingent upon the financial condition of the firm, its

TABLE 5
SOURCES OF FUNDS FOR INVESTMENT BY INDUSTRY, 1955–64

1955-59			%		
	Bonds	Stock		Loans	
			Private	Long-Term Credit Banks	Public
Total	3.3	14.1	62.1	18.6	20.5
Electricity	5.2	11.1	49.1	15.4	34.6
Iron & steel	6.2	29.8	59.3	28.8	4.8
Shipping	0.1	11.4	62.9	19.4	25.6
Coal	1.1	15.9	49.0	42.1	34.0
Textiles	3.6	8.6	74.2	25.0	13.6
Chemicals	2.9	17.2	71.8	28.9	8.2
Ceramics	0.8	17.3	68.3	6.8	13.6
Machinery	5.3	32.3	52.2	25.0	10.2
Non-ferrous metal	2.4	13.2	64.5	21.7	19.9
Land transport -ation	7.7	14.3	62.3	18.3	15.7
Agriculture & fishery	0.4	4.0	44.8	9.6	50.7
Others	1.8	8.5	75.2	11.2	14.5

1960-64			%		
Total	5.6	16.0	64.1	15.4	14.4
Electricity	16.3	12.8	51.3	12.7	19.6
Iron & steel	9.8	30.5	56.2	19.2	3.4
Shipping	0.0	3.8	47.8	12.9	48.5
Coal	1.8	3.2	38.2	23.3	56.8
Textiles	7.4	13.1	66.4	20.6	13.1
Chemicals	4.4	22.4	66.4	21.8	6.8
Ceramics	2.6	17.6	68.9	22.0	11.0
Machinery	7.2	27.6	57.0	19.0	8.1
Non-ferrous metal	3.0	15.9	65.6	21.6	15.8
Land transport- ation	8.8	12.5	60.4	13.4	18.3
Agriculture & fishery	0.6	3.2	48.7	5.7	47.5
Others	1.3	10.3	76.7	11.5	11.7

Source: Japanese Development Bank.

stage of development, and relations between firms and other financiers, between the latter and the main bank, and between the main bank and the regulatory authorities.[9] The nature of bank–firm relationships in the post-war high growth period can be checked alongside the historical statistics. A data set can be gathered from the Securities Report (*Yukashoken Hokokusho*) and a number of directories.[10] In the manufacturing industries, there were 239 firms which specified their debts in 1955, 1965, and 1975. Most of the literature on the main bank system concentrates on the debts carried by firms. One of the city banks was the largest creditor to 50–60 per cent of the 239 companies (Table 6). In other words, it had the largest share in the explicit or implicit loan consortia that supported these manufacturers. The long-term credit banks or trust banks were the second largest contributors. It is worth noting that

TABLE 6
BANK-FIRM RELATIONSHIPS I: LINKS WITH CREDITORS

	Total	City Bank	Long-Term Credit Bank	Trust Bank	Insurance Company	Other
1955						
A	239	141	50	19	8	21
B	121	86	13	8	6	8
C	55	45	6	0	2	2
1965						
A	239	121	41	46	5	26
B	159	97	21	30	3	8
C	77	55	16	4	1	1
1975						
A	239	126	46	40	2	25
B	207	122	38	37	2	8
C	120	83	17	8	2	10
1955-65						
D	116	85	20	8	1	2
1965-75						
D	142	83	29	21	2	7

Notes: A = number of firms classified by the categories of financial institutions to which they owed the largest debt
B = number of firms whose largest creditor was amongst their top ten shareholders, classified according to financial institution
C = number of firms with a director dispatched from their largest creditor, classified according to financial institution
D = number of firms whose largest creditor did not change from 1955–65 or from 1965–75, classified according to financial institution

the number of firms which maintained their links with their largest creditors were smaller than might be expected from the accepted interpretation of these connections, particularly in the years 1955 to 1965.[11] More than half of the sample altered their financing arrangements. Furthermore, in 1955, the largest creditors of almost half the firms were not amongst their top ten shareholders, and almost three-quarters of them did not dispatch directors to their firms' boards. Yet these are supposed to be the conditions by which the main banks monitored their clients and harmonised potentially conflicting interests.[12] The high changeability of the largest creditors and the low ratio of shareholding and interlocking seems to indicate that the main bank system was not solid nor pervasive in the latter half of the 1950s and in the first half of the 1960s.

The prevailing arrangements of this period resulted, to a substantial extent, from the division of work between short-term and long-term financial institutions. To examine this point, another data set is needed. From the above 239 firms, information on the short-term and long-term debts of 89 enterprises were available. Tables 7 and 8 demonstrate the results, and their impact on bank–firm relationships. Even during the rapid growth of 1955 to 1965, some 52 of the 89 firms (or 58 per cent) stayed with their short-term creditors. With regard to long-term creditors, the ratio was only 34 per cent. It is also remarkable that different financial institutions provided short-term and long-term loans. Most of the largest short-term creditors were the city banks, while the majority of the largest long-term creditors were the long-term credit banks and trust banks. The high turnover of long-term creditors and fluctuation in the ratio of long-term loans to short-term loans help explain the weak links between companies and their most important banks (see Table 6 and paragraph above).

Far more than long-term lenders, it was short-term creditors which became the large shareholders of client firms, and it is these institutions which appointed directors. It was not the largest creditor but the largest short-term creditor that was closer to the ideal type of main bank described in the theoretical literature. This implies that the role of the main banks, in many cases city banks, were complemented by the long-term financial institutions. It is worth noting that, even in the case of short-term lenders, the ratio of firms whose top ten shareholders included their largest creditors amounted to only 56 per cent, and that only 29 per cent of them had directors dispatched from their largest creditors (Table 7). Shareholding and interlocking were useful to both the firm and its main bank, but they were by no means indispensable.

The role of main bank imposed heavy burdens on the city banks. They diversified their loans and obligations through consortia and the

TABLE 7
BANK-FIRM RELATIONSHIPS II: LINKS WITH SHORT-TERM CREDITORS

	Total	City Bank	Long-Term Credit Bank	Trust Bank	Insurance Company	Other
1955						
A	89	65	13	2	2	7
B	50	39	5	1	2	3
C	26	24	1	0	0	1
1965						
A	89	69	3	1	1	15
B	60	55	2	1	1	1
C	36	34	1	0	1	0
1975						
A	89	82	4	0	1	2
B	79	75	3	0	0	1
C	58	54	3	0	0	1
1955-65						
D	52	49	3	0	0	0
1965-75						
D	64	63	1	0	0	0

Notes: A = number of firms classified by the categories of financial institutions to which they owed the largest short-term debt
    B = number of firms whose largest short-term creditor was amongst their top ten shareholders, classified according to financial institution
    C = number of firms with a director dispatched from their largest short-term creditor, classified according to financial institution
    D = number of firms whose largest short-term creditor did not change from 1955–65 or from 1965–75, classified according to financial institution

co-operation of long-term financial institutions, but an aggregated balance sheet of their position indicates genuine difficulties (Table 9). The composition of both assets and liabilities changed dramatically from the pre-war to the post-war period. The ratio of securities, especially government bonds, decreased, while that of credits increased. As a result, the liquidity of their assets declined substantially. The head of the credit analysis section at the Daiichi Bank (one of the big six city banks) wrote in 1956 that 'the present bank assets differ greatly from those of the pre-war period' and that the 'decline in the ratio of government bonds, the very best assets, indicates above all the decline in the quality of banks' financial position.'[13] Worse still, the ratio of capital liabilities to total liabilities had also fallen since before the war, and this change was a cause of similar concern.[14] The overall deterioration in liquidity

TABLE 8
BANK–FIRM RELATIONSHIPS III: LINKS WITH LONG-TERM CREDITORS

	Total	City Bank	Long-Term Credit Bank	Trust Bank	Insurance Company	Other
1955						
A	89	10	44	24	8	3
B	16	0	2	8	6	0
C	4	2	2	0	0	0
1965						
A	89	6	33	41	6	3
B	48	6	10	27	4	1
C	12	3	5	4	0	0
1975						
A	89	9	37	37	5	1
B	69	9	28	26	5	1
C	20	8	7	3	2	0
1955-65						
D	30	2	19	8	1	0
1965-75						
D	60	3	27	28	2	0

Notes: A = number of firms classified by the categories of financial institutions to which they owed the largest long-term debt
B = number of firms whose largest long-term creditor was amongst their top ten shareholders, classified according to financial institution
C = number of firms with a director dispatched from their largest long-term creditor, classified according to financial institution
D = number of firms whose largest long-term creditor did not change from 1955–65 or from 1965–75, classified according to financial institution

damaged their ability to bear risks, and, while causing instability in the financial system, it could have choked off funds to industries. It is not surprising that, since the 1950s, the 'over loan problem' – excessive bank loans depending on the backing of the BOJ – became a matter of widespread discussion in financial circles, governments, and the press. Several measures of reform had to be imposed on the city banks, and institutional arrangements complementary to the main bank system had to be evolved, these being reliant on the regulation of funds allocation by MOF and MITI, the long-term credit banks, the JDB, and the control of bonds issues.

The regulation of the city banks had to comply with the investment needs of the industrial policy devised by MITI and the MOF. Guidelines for the bank management and the allocation of bank loans were key

TABLE 9
BALANCE SHEET OF CITY BANKS

	1935	1944	1950	% 1955	1960	1965	1970
Assets:							
Currency & deposits	6.9	4.7	11.6	12.3	11.2	10.3	9.0
Call money	4.7	0.3	0.0	0.3	0.0	0.0	0.0
Securities	35.5	27.7	5.9	9.2	11.4	·12.4	10.7
Government bonds	19.5	23.9	2.3	1.3	0.4	0.1	0.9
Local govn. bonds	3.8	0.2	0.0	0.5	0.9	1.2	1.4
Industrial bonds	10.7	3.3	3.3	6.2	8.1	9.0	5.9
Stocks	1.5	0.8	0.3	1.1	1.9	2.1	2.4
Loans & credits	42.7	63.3	50.1	56.7	59.3	57.5	58.9
Loans	35.5	61.6	33.1	33.4	36.8	37.7	38.9
Discounted bills	7.2	1.7	17.1	23.3	22.5	19.9	20.1
Liabilities:							
Demand deposits	23.2	27.6	30.6	31.0	23.2	21.7	18.5
Time deposits	58.0	37.7	18.7	36.8	41.5	39.8	43.6
Loans	0.0	16.1	9.2	2.6	7.2	8.3	7.3
Foreign exchange	0.7	0.0	12.9	1.2	3.3	3.5	2.8
Call money	0.0	0.0	0.3	2.3	3.0	4.9	5.5
Capital	14.6	3.9	2.8	2.8	3.8	3.3	3.9

Source: Bank of Japan, *Keizai Tokei Nenpo* (*Annual Report of Economic Statistics*).

policy issues for the MOF until the first half of the 1960s, involving the stabilisation of bank management (*kenzenka*) and qualitative credit adjustment (*shitsuteki shin'yo chosei*).[15] Measures designed to influence commercial practice were regulations on interest rates, the opening of bank branches, and performance indices. MOF sought to avoid the bankruptcy of any bank, the so-called 'convoy policy' (*Goso Sendan Gyosei*). The Temporary Interest Rates Adjustment Law (*Rinji Shikin Chosei Ho*) was introduced in 1947, and maximum returns on deposits and loans were to be decided by the MOF in accordance with BOJ's Policy Board.[16] The controls afforded the banks a positive profit margin of between one and two per cent in the 1950s, while it had been about 0.5 per cent in the pre-war years (see Bank of Japan's *Annual Report on Economic Statistics*). As well as the 'price' of interest rates, non-price competition was also curtailed by controls on the opening of branches and entry into the banking sector. Under the Banking Law (*Ginko Ho*), the MOF did not sanction any entrant and the number of institutions has remained stable since 1952.[17] Businesses attracted by the increased profits to be made in banking were prevented from destabilising the industry, just as existing institutions could not open branches that disrupted the activities of rivals.[18] The MOF was equally determined that the additional profits and rents assisted the stabilisation of the financial sector and the welfare of depositors.[19] It had therefore to set a number of performance indices. First, the Ministry in 1949 set a guideline ratio of ordinary expenses to ordinary income. In August 1953, a letter from the chief of MOF's banking section issued clear instructions that any surplus should be used to boost reserves, reduce the interest rates on loans, or increase the returns on deposits.[20] The distribution of profits to shareholders was restricted through the regulation of dividend payments.

There were, in addition, questions of industrial policy. Since the Temporary Law on Funds Allocation Control of 1937 (*Rinji Shikin Chosei Ho*), and the Rules on Funds Allocation by Financial Institutions of 1937 (*Kin'yu Kikan Shikin Yuzu Junsoku*), the MOF and the BOJ had overseen the granting of finance by private banks.[21] Although direct controls had been abolished after the war, the MOF still gave administrative guidance to a system of voluntary regulation. In 1951, the government announced a series of policies intended to restrain inflation, supply funds to strategic industries, and limit the financing of 'unnecessary' sectors. The MOF issued a notice setting out instructions for the granting of loans, and the National Federation of Banking Associations (NFBA, or *Zenkoku Ginko Kyokai Rengokai*) formed a Committee for the Self-Regulation of Loans (*Yushi Jishukisei Iinkai*), charged with 'examining loans to be restrained, announcing criteria, and providing guidelines for the discretion of each bank'.[22] At first, in July 1951, the committee chose to limit funds for building, real estate, and public amusements, and in 1953 loans for speculation and excessive or duplicate investment were rigidly restrained.[23] Then the institutions overseeing this system of indirect control were substantially extended, at a time when macro-economic policy was tightened between 1954 and 1957 in a response to trade imbalances. In 1954, the MOF informed all the banks that, in addition to limiting so-called unnecessary loans, they should give priority to key parts of the economy and an improvement in exports.[24] In other words, the Ministry wanted private banks through self-regulation to concentrate their financing on the strategic industries of coal, iron and steel, electricity, and shipping, just as public funds were being targeted. The ruling Democratic and Liberal Parties were also seeking to reduce the pressure on public funds, which were in short supply. They therefore planned to regulate directly the allocation of bank funds by law, and drew up a draft Funds Committee Law (*Shikin linkai Ho*) in 1955. When financial and business circles became strongly opposed, the MOF withdrew its support, and the legislation was never enacted. As a substitute, the Council on the Funds of Financial Institutions (*Kin'yu Kikan Shikin Shingikai*) was established in 1956 to discuss and co-ordinate the allocation of funds by private financial institutions, and it contained representatives from finance, business, academics, and civil servants.[25]

In the meantime, the NFBA had extended the reach of self-regulation with the aim of invalidating the Funds Committee Law, during a period when the proposal was still current. In 1955, it established the Committee for Investment and Loans (*Toyushi Iinkai*),[26] and this new body assisted the funding of industries identified by the government as strategic. The Committee, composed of the presidents and directors of major banks, and representatives from the MOF and BOJ, discussed loan policies in relation to key economic sectors and the provision of public finance.[27] The MOF and the NFBA agreed to work in fulfilment of the Five Year Plan for the Independence of the Japanese Economy (*Keizai Jiritsu Gokanen Keikaku*), drawn up in 1955.[28] As macro-economic policy continued to be tightened, further developments in the public and private sectors followed. In June 1957, a cabinet meeting decided on the Emergency Measures against the Imbalance of Trade Payments, and the restraint of unnecessary investments was emphasised. The MOF instructed the banks to give priority to strategic industries, and they were told to minimise the levels of funds even to these sectors.[29] To implement the policy, the NFBA merged its Committee for Investment and Loans and the Committee for the Self-Regulation of Loans. The Committee for the Regulation of Funds Allocation (*Shikin Chosei Iinkai*) was formed, and under it a Managerial Meeting for the Regulation of Funds Allocation (*Shikin Chosei Kanjikai*) was appointed.[30] During these events, institutional arrangements to secure the co-operation of industries were planned, and, in 1957, a working committee representing finance, business, and the civil service was created under the Council on the Funds of Financial Institutions. Delegates from the Tokyo Chamber of Commerce, the Federation of Business Associations, the Electricity Association, the Japan Iron and Steel Association, the Coal Association, and the Chemical Association represented business, and this small committee had a role in co-ordinating funds allocation and the investment plans of manufacturers.[31] Co-ordination between the financial and industrial sectors was finally systemised in December 1957 through the establishment of the Funds Branch of the Council on Industrial Rationalisation

(*Sangyo Gorika Shingikai Sangyo Shikin Bukai*) at MITI.[32] It consisted
of representatives from the Federation of Business Associations, NFBA,
JDB, IBJ, and several business organisations and large companies.
Reviewing the work of the Council on the Funds of Financial Institutions and the NFBA's Committee for the Regulation of Funds
Allocation, the new Funds Branch adjusted and co-ordinated the investment plans of industries. These loan policies were first prepared by
the respective bureau at MITI (*genkyoku*), framed through discussion
with each industry's business association. After the adjustments of
the Funds Branch, negotiations between industries and *genkyoku* were
repeated in an iterative manner. The banks secured high quality information on the direction of industrial policy at MITI and sanctioned
investment projects, and their loans were gradually adjusted according
to official priorities. When the Council on Industrial Rationalisation was
transformed in 1964 into the Council on Industrial Structure (*Sangyo
Kozo Shingikai*), the Funds Branch was continued.[33]

IV

LONG-TERM FINANCIAL INSTITUTIONS AND THE
BONDS MARKET

Other measures were taken to secure the stability of the financial system
and the supply of funds to the strategic industries. First, public funds
were provided to relieve the shortage of long-term finance to business.
The Reconstruction Finance Corporation (RFC, or *Fukko Kinyu
Kinko*) had had an important role since 1947, but was ordered by the
US's General Headquarters in 1949 to cease lending new funds.
The RFC's substitute, the USAID Counterpart Fund, proved insufficient, and its special clients in the coal, iron and steel, shipping, and
electricity industries were especially hindered, despite their strategic
role. As a result, the Japan Development Bank was founded in 1950.[34]
The JDB had to assist the government's industrial policy, whilst
exercising its own independent judgement in each case. The framework
was determined by the Basic Policy for Loans (*Un'yo Kihon Hoshin*),
as decided by a cabinet meeting for every fiscal year. In 1952,
the electricity, shipping, coal, iron and steel, chemical, machinery,
agriculture, fishing, and synthetic fibre industries were deemed to be
strategic.[35] Following the basic policy, and relying on information from
the funds branch at the Council on Industrial Rationalisation, the JDB
examined the creditworthiness of each project. During the 1950s, coal,
iron and steel, electricity, and shipping received continuous support,

and, after that, more attention was paid to regional development. From the beginning, the JDB explored joint loans with the private banks.[36] JDB loans were 'cow bells', signalling whether a project met the twin objectives of industrial policy and individual creditworthiness.[37]

Two years after the JDB, in 1952, the Long-Term Credit Bank Law was passed. The Industrial Bank of Japan (IBJ) was reorganised, and the Long-Term Credit Bank of Japan was founded. These institutions were expected to supply long-term funds to officially determined strategic industries, and the bank debentures which they issued enjoyed an advantage as collateral for all those seeking BOJ credit. As we have noted, the credit banks played a complementary role to the main bank system, offering long-term finance to the short-term provision of the city banks. Moreover, the large part of bank debentures issued by the credit banks were held by the city banks, although the interest rates on these debentures were lower than those to be gained through loans. In addition to providing collateral for the BOJ, the city banks expected the long-term credit banks to lend money to their customers in industry.[38] The LCBJ wrote that 'We supplied long-term funds to the client firms of the commercial banks which were the main holders of our bank debentures in order to relieve those bank burdens, and we also take care to make the funds return to those banks as deposits'.[39]

The corporate bonds market was another means of long-term funds. Their promotion began with the regulation of the financial institutions by the Bank of Japan after 1949, and the BOJ took two measures in order to effect this policy. First, it screened and rated the bonds that qualified as collateral for its credit *ex ante*, and in practice only these could be issued. Second, when a bank bought bonds, the BOJ purchased an equal sum in government bonds from that bank.[40] As the interest rate of BOJ credit was substantially lower than the market rate, both measures acted as *de facto* subsidies to the banks.[41] The bank regulated the interest rate and the level of bond issues through the Conference on Bonds Issue (*Kisai Kondankai*) and the Consultation Meeting on Bonds Issue (*Kisai Uchiawasekai*). The former consisted of the MOF, BOJ, the entrusting banks, and the big four securities companies, and these decided on bonds issue policy. The latter, composed of BOJ, the entrusting banks, and the big four securities companies, set the conditions for respective issues.[42] Through the regulation of the bonds market, strategic industries could be given priority, and, although *ex ante* screening and rating was abolished in 1956, the Consultation Meeting on Bonds Issue continued to be influential.[43] The entrusting banks, members of the Consultation Meeting, maintained good contacts with the Committee for the Self-Regulation of Loans and the

Committee for Investment and Loans at the NFBA, in order to ensure that the banks held the bonds of strategic industries.[44] Furthermore, they not only advised the issuing firms, but also monitored them on behalf of bond holders, and it was natural for the main banks to assume this role. We can examine all the bonds issued by our sample of 89 firms between 1960 and 1965 (see above). In 439 of 489 cases (that is about 90 per cent), the main banks, which were the largest short-term creditors in 1965, took part in entrusting. As to those companies whose main banks were also city banks, the ratio was nearer 100 per cent, the issuing of bonds complementing the system of main banks (see Table 10).

TABLE 10
BONDS ENTRUSTED WITH MAIN BANK

	No. of Firms	No. of Bonds Issues	No. of Cases Main Bank Entrusted with Bonds Issues
Total	54	489	431
IBJ	2	4	4
Mitsui Bank	9	102	102
Mitsubishi Bank	4	42	42
Sumitomo Bank	5	73	73
Fuji Bank	7	68	68
Sanwa Bank	4	29	29
Daiichi Bank	5	68	68
Kangyo Bank	5	28	28
Tokai Bank	1	3	3
Kyowa Bank	2	16	14
Norinchukin Bank	9	48	0
Foreign Bank	1	8	0

Source: Industrial Bank of Japan, *Shasai Ichiran (Lists of Industrial Bonds)* (Tokyo, 1970).

V

THE JAPANESE FINANCIAL SYSTEM AND COMPETITIVE ADVANTAGE

The Japanese financial system in the high growth era was one of complementary institutions, which involved the main banks, long-term finance institutions, and financial regulation and industrial policy. The main banks co-ordinated explicit and implicit loan consortia which supplied funds to client firms, and in this objective they were assisted by funds from the long-term finance institutions, bond market regulation by the BOJ, bank regulation by the MOF, and the funds allocations of the MOF and MITI. There was a characteristic division of labour within Japan's financial system in the post-war period. Aoki *et al.* argued that many financial functions – the monitoring of companies and their investment projects *ex ante*, *interim*, and *ex post* – were carried out by the main banks in an integrative manner, and that the main banks' *ex ante* monitoring was supported by that of public financial institutions, long-term credit banks, and government councils such as the Council for Co-ordinating Electric Energy Source Development.[45] We have shown that this structure was true of not just the electricity industry, a public utility under rigid government control, but of all industries. Aoki *et al.* also underrated the role of the MOF and MITI, carried out through the Council on the Funds of Financial Institutions and the Funds Branch of the Council on Industrial Rationalisation, in co-ordinating and screening investment in industry.

How well did this system perform? It is well known that Japanese industries grew rapidly in the post-war period, and that they depended on funds borrowed from financial institutions. The system was highly influenced and shaped by the recognition, expectation and behaviour of the agents which composed it. The head of the credit analysis section of Daiichi Bank wrote in 1956 that 'it is said that depositors' thinking has been changing since the end of the war. They may confide only in the banks because they are banks'.[46] The MOF's 'convoy policy' had removed any element of risk. In 1959, the head of MOF's banking division wrote that 'it cannot be denied that the banks have to some extent lost consciousness of how they are entrusted with depositors' funds because they are confident in banks not being bankrupted.[47] Regulation also altered perspectives of industrial enterprises. In 1962, the president of the Fuji Iron and Steel Company said that 'I suppose that the rationing of funds itself encourages a demand for large-scale financing, because the industries feel that the projects to which the funds are allocated are authorised by the government'.[48] Government regulation and co-ordination of the financial system stimulated investment in industrial firms, as did its willingness to limit in effect entry into a number of sectors. In 1965, the president of the Petrochemical Association said that the projects planned by many firms were encouraged by these controls, because, if a firm obtained government permission for the investment, it could expect future limitations on the right of entry into that sector.[49] It was this alteration in outlook and attitude that stimulated large-scale investment and high-speed growth. Nonetheless, there were historical circumstances that enabled the system to function well in post-war Japan. Close bank–industry and government–firm relations already existed, and, in the push to overcome economic backwardness, it was relatively easy to agree on strategically important industries. The experiences of the Japanese 'bubble' economy in the 1980s, and its subsequent bursting, revealed faults in a financial system that had not adjusted to the realities of a developed nation.

NOTES

1. See Masahiko Aoki and Hugh Patrick (eds.), *The Japanese Main Bank System and its Relevance for Developing Markets and Transforming Socialist Economies* (Oxford, forthcoming); Akiyoshi Horiuchi and Qing-yuan Sui, 'Mein Banku Kankei no Keizai Bunseki: Tenbo' ('Economic Analysis of the Main Bank System: A Survey'), Discussion Paper (University of Tokyo), 92-J-1, 1992.
2. Masahiko Aoki, 'Historical Conditions for Monitoring Roles of the Japanese Main Bank System', forthcoming in Aoki and Patrick, *Japanese Main Bank System*; Kazuo Ueda, 'Institutional and Regulatory Frameworks for Main Bank System', forthcoming in ibid.
3. For an outline of the post-war Japanese financial system, see Koichi Hamada and Akiyoshi Horiuch, 'The Political Economy of the Financial Market', in Kozo Yamamura and Yasykichi Yasuba (eds.), *The Political Economy of Japan*, Vol.1 (Stanford, 1987).
4. Hiroshi Yoshikawa and Tetsuji Okazaki, 'Postwar Hyper-Inflation and the Dodge Plan: An Overview', in Yutaka Kosai and Juro Teranishi (eds.), *The Japanese Experience of Economic Reforms* (London 1993).
5. Yoshio Suzuki (ed.), *The Japanese Financial System* (Oxford, 1987), pp.171–2.
6. Ibid., pp.200–203.
7. Ibid., pp.163–4.
8. Masahiko Aoki, Hugh Patrick, and Paul Sheard, 'The Japanese Main Bank System: An Introductory Overview', in Aoki and Patrick, *Japanese Main Bank System*, p.4.
9. Ibid., pp.4–5.
10. Tokyo Shoken Torihikijo, *Jojo Kaisha Soran (Prospectus of Listed Companies) (1956 version); Kiezai Chosa Kyokai,* Nenpo Keiretsu no Kenkyu (Annual Report of Research on Keiretsu) (1966 version); Toyo Kiezai Shinposha, *Kigyo Keiretsu Soran (Directory of Keiretsu)* (1976 version).
11. On the changeability of main banks, see Yoshiro Miwa, 'Mein Banku to sono Kino' ('The Main Bank and its Function'), in Talkafusa Nakamura *et al.*(eds.), *Gendai Nihon no Keizai Shisutemu (The Economic System of Contemporary Japan)* (Tokyo 1985); Shinichi Hirota, 'Nihon ni okeru Mein Banku no Koteisei ni Tsuite' ('On the Fixity of the Main Bank in Japan'), *Keizaigaku Ronso*, Vol.41 No.2 (1989); Horiuchi and Sui, *Main Bank System*, pp.22–3.
12. Horiuchi and Sui, *Main Bank System*, pp.6–7.
13. Kaoru Inoue, 'Ginko Shisan no Seijoka ni tusite' ('On the Normalization of Bank Assets'), *Kin'yu* (Oct. 1956), pp.5–6.
14. Ibid., p.5.
15. MOF (ed.), *Showa Zaisei Shi: 1952–1973 (Financial History of Showa Era: 1952–1973)*, Vol.10, pp.76–7.
16. Ibid., pp.118–22.
17. Ibid., pp.95–8.
18. Ibid., p.80.
19. Ibid., p.80; Ueda, 'Institutional and Regulatory Frameworks', pp.9–10.
20. MOF (ed.), *Financial History*, Vol.110, pp.80–81.
21. Tetsuji Okazaki and Masahiro Okuno-Fujiwara, 'Gendai Nihon no Keizai Shisutemu to sono Rekishiteki Genryu' ('The Contemporary Japanese Economic System and its

Historical Origins'), in Testuji Okazaki and Masahiro Okuno-Fujiwara (eds.), *Gendai Nihon Keizai Shisutemu no Genryu (Historical Origins of the Contemporary Japanese Economic System) (Tokyo, 1993), pp.18, 30–31.*
22. *NFBA,* Ginko Kyokai Nijunen Shi (20 Years History of NFBA) (Tokyo 1965), pp.61–2.
23. Ibid., pp.163–4.
24. Banking Bureau of MOF, *Year Book of Financial Affairs (Ginko Kyoku Kin'yu Nenpo)* (1955 version), pp.21–3.
25. Ibid., (1956 version), pp.44–6; NFBA *20 Years History,* pp.191–2.
26. NFBA, *20 Years History,* p.193.
27. *Kin'yu* (1955), p.71.
28. Banking Bureau of MOF, *Year Book* (1956 version), pp.52–3.
29. Ibid., (1958 version), pp.29–30.
30. NFBA, *20 Years History,* p.339.
31. Banking Bureau of MOF, *Year Book* (1958 version), pp.36–8.
32. MITI (ed.), *Tsusho Sangyo Seisaku Shi (History of the Trade and Industrial Policy),* Vol.6, pp.349, 353.
33. A detailed study on the Funds Branch of the Council on Industrial Rationalization is being prepared by Tetsui Okazaki, Masahiro Okuno-Fujiwara (University of Tokyo) and Kaz'uo Ueda (University of Tokyo).
34. JDB, *Nihon Kaihatsu Ginko Nijugonen Shi (25 Years History of JDB),* (Tokyo, 1976), pp.40–41.
35. Ibid., p.50.
36. Ibid., p.55.
37. Mikinari Higano, *Kin'yu Kikan no Shinsa Noryoku (The Credit Analysis Capability of Financial Institutions)* (Tokyo, 1986), pp.67–87; Horiuchi and Sui, 'The Influence of Japan Development Bank Loans on Corporate Investment Behaviour' University of Tokyo, Discussion Paper Series, 93-F-12, 1993, pp.6–10.
38. Kaichi Shimura, *Gendai Nihon Koshasai Ron (A Study of Public and Private Bonds in Contemporary Japan)* (Tokyo, 1978), p.137.
39. LCTB, *Nihon Choki Shin'yo Ginko Junen Shi (10 Years History of LCTB)* (Tokyo, 1962), pp.141–2.
40. Yamaichi Securities and Yamaichi Institute of Economic Research, *Wagakuni Kigyo no Shikin Chotatsu (Corporate Finance in Japan)* (Tokyo 1977) p.18.
41. Juro Teranishi, *Nihon no Keizai Hatten to Kin'yu (Japanese Economic Development and the Financial System)* (Tokyo, 1993), Ch.8.
42. Ibid., p.210.
43. Shimura, *A Study of Public and Private Bonds,* p.114.
44. Ibid., p.126.
45. Aoki, 'Historical Conditions', pp.10–13.
46. Inoue, 'Normalisation of Bank Assets', p.8.
47. Tadao Shiotani, 'Tomen no Ginko Gyosei no Mondaiten' ('Issues of Present Banking Policy'), *Kin'yu* (Oct. 1959).
48. 'Zadankai: Keizai no Genjo to Keizai Unei no Hoko' ('A Symposium: Present Economy and the Direction of Economic Policy'), *Keidanren Geppo* (June 1962).
49. 'Zadankai: Toshi Chosei wo Do Susumeru ka' ('A Symposium: How Should We Adjust Investment Plans?'), *Keidanren Geppo* (April 1965).

The Development of Production Management at the Toyota Motor Corporation

MASARU UDAGAWA
Hosei University

The brilliant debut of the Japanese automobile industry into world markets was assisted by the two oil crises of the 1970s which brought about soaring petrol prices and a rapid shift in demand towards smaller cars. During this period, the Japanese car industry coped with dramatic changes in the world economy, and expanded its production by increasing exports to other countries, mainly the USA. In other words, it was already equipped with a production system and quality control programme which enabled it to overcome the turmoil and structural adjustments of the 1970s, and this advantage in international competitiveness made its enlargement of world market share possible. Reflecting a growing interest in the remarkable development of this industry, many studies have been undertaken in recent years, and the interests of scholars, particularly Western ones,[1] have concentrated on the specific characteristics of production systems. The purpose of this paper is to give an historical overview of the strategy and management of the Toyota Motor Corporation, now the largest Japanese car manufacturer, and second in the world only to General Motors, so demonstrating how it formed and established its production system and quality control programme to such a degree of competitive advantage. To highlight the characteristics of Toyota's system, comparisons will be made with the Nissan Motor Corporation, its greatest rival. The policies adopted by Toyota and later imitated by Nissan in the area of production management during the 1950s and 1960s were to provide both companies with organisational capabilities that proved increasingly superior to overseas competitors.

II

THE 'FIVE-YEAR' PLAN AND STATISTICAL CONTROL

The procurement boom which followed the outbreak of the Korean War in 1950 helped Toyota overcome its business difficulties and secured a basis for its reconstruction. Utilising this lucrative stream of profits, Toyota began in April 1951 its 'five-year plan for the modernisation of production facilities'. The purpose of this plan, involving a Y5,787 million investment, was to establish a mass production system using the latest machinery and advanced factory layout.[2] There was a particular reason for Toyota's rapid move towards the renewal of equipment and the implementation of large-scale production. In October 1949, the General Headquarters of the Allied Forces (GHQ) had deregulated the manufacture of passenger cars. In response, Japanese makers began to search for alliances with foreign companies in order to fill, in a short period, the technological gap which had resulted in part from the production ban on passenger cars during the war period. Toyota also planned an overseas link and started negotiations with Ford Motors in June 1950. The Korean War broke out in the same month and the US Department of Defense restricted outward investment and the dispatch of American engineers overseas. The two companies were forced to halt negotiations.[3] Toyota wondered if it could survive as a passenger car manufacturer, and top management announced that it would return to its founding philosophy, the development and application of a national technology. In January 1952, it began designing a new, indigenous passenger car,[4] and this decision had important repercussions for the company and its industry in the adoption and adaption of production organisation. The five-year plan was a natural consequence of its failure to obtain foreign technology.[5]

Meanwhile, military procurement during the Korean conflict not only facilitated Toyota's sluggish recovery after the Second World War but also made it acutely conscious of quality control issues. In the early 1950s, Toyota's product quality could not satisfy the stipulated requirements of the US Army,[6] but it soon came to appreciate the gap which existed between American and Japanese operating techniques. In 1951, Toyota began to receive advice from quality control experts in the US Army and introduced Statistical Quality Control (SQC) methods to their production processes. In 1953, the company established an overall Quality Control Section within its Inspection Department and made it responsible for the design of inspection tools, the exact measurement of raw materials, parts and products, and other related activities. In the autumn of the same year, Toyota founded a Quality Control Committee to oversee the whole works, and the Personnel Department in co-operation with the Quality Control Section invited experts to provide training for employees in control chart methods, experimental designs, and sampling inspection.[7] Despite these efforts, Toyota's quality control activities in the 1950s did not in practice always involve the workers in the manufacturing departments. This was mainly due to its QC methods being too statistical in their nature and being unsuited to the 'assuring of quality in each process' by all concerned. Indeed, the approach enhanced the traditional, engrained belief that thorough inspection alone could improve quality.[8]

III

THE BEGINNINGS OF TQC AND KANBAN

In January 1955, Toyota launched its first fully fledged national passenger car, the Crown, and a small-sized four-wheel truck, the Toyoace, both of which proved to be moderate successes. Then, immediately after the completion of the five-year plan for the modernising of production facilities in March 1956, Toyota extended an existing plant in Koromo, near Nagoya. In 1958, it started the construction of the Motomachi plant, also near Nagoya and the first exclusive plant for passenger car manufacture in Japan. It was completed in the following year. In the meantime, the company foresaw growth in the small car market and launched the Corolla series in 1957. Under the five-year plan, Toyota tried to take the lead from companies reliant on foreign technology and advice. It continued to modernise its plant equipment by so-called 'catalogue engineering', largely the installation of machines and equipment ordered from foreign catalogues.[9] The favourable effects of mass production and plant modernisation were realised following the rapid rise in demand for cars in Japan, which occurred with the launch of the Crown. As a result, Toyota's annual production in 1959 reached 100,000 units, the first time such a target had been reached by a Japanese car manufacturer (see Table 1).

When Toyota received an order in 1958 from the US Army Procurement Agency (APA) in Japan, to be fulfilled by the beginning of the next year, greater through-put did not bring about the expected gains in cost reduction, productivity and quality improvement.[10] Nor could the administration departments keep pace with rising production,[11] and the management system gradually slackened. Between 1958 and 1962 there was a series of unpredicted events. Firstly, Toyota had to review its quality control system for parts, including the procedures of its suppliers. It was being forced to satisfy the quality standards of the APA, which at the time were more exacting than Toyota's. Secondly, when the company began to export its Crown model to the United States in 1958, the problems of body overweight, power shortage and high-speed instability soon became obvious. In 1960, when Nissan was increasing

TABLE 1
TOYOTA PRODUCTION (000 VEHICLES)

Year	Cars	Trucks	Buses	Total
1955	7	15	0.2	23
1960	42	112	0.5	155
1965	236	239	2.1	478
1970	1068	524	16.6	1609
1975	1715	609	12.3	2336
1980	2303	954	35.9	3293
1985	2569	1058	38.1	3666

Source: Nihon Jidosha Kogyokai (Japan Automobile Manufacturers' Association) (ed.), *Jidōsha Tōkei Geppou* (*Automobile Statistics Monthly*) (1955–85).

the sales of its Bluebird in the US market, Toyota had to halt exports of the Crown. Thirdly, technological problems were discovered in the New Corona, which was launched in 1959. This model had been restyled largely from the original Corona in order to compete against Nissan's Bluebird, but Toyota was completely defeated in the first 'BC (Bluebird versus Corona) War'.[12] When it withdrew from the USA, Toyota had to surrender its position as leading exporter in passenger cars to its rival. In addition to problems overseas, the liberalisation of finished imports was imminent.[13]

In order to tackle mounting troubles at home and abroad, and to reconstruct a slackened management system, Toyota implemented two programmes. One was the introduction of Total Quality Control (TQC) and the other was the company-wide use of the *Kanban* system. When Toyota received the APA's orders in May 1959, it changed the name of its Inspection Department to the Quality Control Department, and charged it with the implementation of TQC. In June of the following year, Eiji Toyoda, the executive vice-president, distributed within the company a pamphlet entitled 'Request for Inspection'. He criticised traditional ways of thinking and the notion that 'strict inspection makes good quality'. He also revealed his thoughts on future policy, saying that 'The ideal inspection is no inspection. If all the machines and equipment can assure the quality of products, inspection becomes unnecessary'.[14] Toyota's TQC programmes were implemented according to this principle. The first phase (June 1961 to December 1962) focused on the achievement of quality and price standards that were internationally competitive. It reviewed and improved departmental operations and management systems, and it tried to make all workers engaged in manufacturing aware of the concept of 'quality assurance in each process'. The campaign strove to reduce by half failures in materials, processing and reworking. The second phase (January 1963 to August 1964) stressed improvements in inter-departmental communication and co-operation, because executives had tended to represent their own department's interests. The other main theme of this phase was the development of the third-generation Corona and the creation of smoothly run production systems. In the third phase (September 1964 to September 1965), the company sought a functional management system in which quality assurance and cost management were the two major pillars. It also applied for the Deming Prize, established in 1950 in honour of Dr W.E. Deming's contribution to quality control activities in post-war Japan, and, as a result, its TQC activities were fully investigated.[15]

Toyota's *Kanban* system,[16] a method of production control, consisted of two chief concepts, namely Just-in-Time (JIT) and *Jidoka* (automation the Toyota way). The former dealt with the arrival of needed components in the needed quantities when they were required at each assembly station. The latter allowed workers on the production line to exercise their own judgement and halt operations when mechanical troubles or other abnormalities occurred. Then they had to find the cause and solve the problem. Such a system completely reversed Fordist theories on deskilling and long production runs. In 1949, Toyota introduced on a test basis a production control system using the concepts of JIT and *Jidoka* in the machine shop at the Koromo plant. In order to implement full-scale JIT production in the machine shop in 1953, Toyota started the *Kanban* system, which was based on supplies being 'pulled' through the production process as and when they were needed, and the approach copied the sales methods of US supermarkets. Further, in 1955 Toyota applied these methods in the assembly and body manufacturing shops. *Kanban* brought various advantages such as the elimination of waste due to the over-production of parts, the maintenance of buffer stocks, and multiplied defects.

Before the start-up of the Motomachi Plant, however, the *Kanban* system was supported only by Eiji Toyoda and a number of executives. Many managers and engineers emphasised the building of a mass production system through the introduction of the latest machinery and equipment, and skilled workers showed resistance to the *Kanban* system. Its application was limited to those plants controlled by Taiichi Ohno, the system's founder, and, since the start of production at the Motomachi plant, Toyota had experienced frequent difficulties. It had to review its production control system and examined conventional reliance on the use of the latest machinery and facilities, but the company continued to depend on technology and day-to-day improvement activities.[17] In 1963, top management decided on the full application of *Kanban* as a means of transforming the production control system. Toyota had to minimise variances in work volume at each process stage so that parts and semi-finished products moved smoothly through the factory. To obtain 'smoothed production', Toyota started a study on the 'single unit production and conveyance' system in which the components on the final assembly line are minimised and the same model is not conveyed consecutively. JIT and smoothed production necessitated a guarantee of good quality parts for each successive process, and Toyota had to pursue the thorough application of *Jidoka* in its plants and a quality assurance procedure for each process. In parallel with the company-wide application of the *Kanban* system, Toyota transferred the parts and raw material inspection function once held by the Quality Control Department at head office to each plant. The main instruments of production control were also devolved. As a result, the *Kanban* system in the plants and the TQC activities of head office, formerly conducted separately, were integrated.[18] Meanwhile, Toyota initiated a QC education programme for all employees. Since 1963, it has regularly held a QC meeting in each operating unit, consisting of first line supervisors such as general foremen, foremen, group leaders, engineers and QC staff. They conducted problem solving activities using QC methods, and since 1964 QC circles have been organised.[19]

IV

SUPPLIER CONTROL

In Japan, the ratio of in-house production at final car assemblers is low. They depend on external parts suppliers for 70 to 80 per cent of their components, in contrast to General Motors' 30 per cent. Therefore, Toyota had to apply *Kanban* not only to its own company but also to transactions with parts suppliers. It had to concentrate too on the quality and performance of the parts supplied by sub-contractors to a level of those produced in-house. When Toyota started its five-year plan, it was analysed by the Manufacturing Industry Guidance Centre and the Industry and Commerce Department of the Aichi Prefecture, and the activities of the company and of parts suppliers was similarly investigated. As a consequence, Toyota began to give advice on modern management and quality control to its suppliers in co-operation with

Kyohokai,[20] which was a co-operative association of its parts manufacturers. After the completion of the five-year plan and the establishment of a mass production system, Toyota began to place a higher priority on volume in its supplier control policy, and this outlook contributed to the Crown's ultimate withdrawal from the US market and its defeat in the 'first BC War'.[21] From this point, TQC activities were introduced and the issue of supplier quality control emerged as the major task. Personnel from the Quality Control Department and the Technical Section of the Purchasing Department visited major parts suppliers between September 1960 and May 1961. It then divided the suppliers into three groups, and began to provide frequent quality control seminars for each of them. In order to vitalise the activities of *Kyohokai*, Toyota sent its own employees to join its committees, which along with the company advised suppliers on management rationalisation and quality control. Since 1964, *Kyohokai*'s annual plan has been based upon Toyota's purchase policy, and new committees for their implementation were established within the suppliers' association.[22]

V

THE COMPLETION OF TOYOTA'S PRODUCTION SYSTEM

In 1963, Toyota regained its top position as a producer of passenger cars from Nissan, and in 1966 overtook its competitor in export markets. In other words, it won the 'second BC War' against Nissan. Immediately after receiving the Deming Prize in 1965, Toyota reaffirmed that TQC activities would continue to be its core means of management control, asserted in the slogan 'All-Toyota Quality Assurance'.[23] In November 1967, the company began its 'zero defect programme' to develop the *Kanban* system one stage further. The QC circles were made the main instruments of production control, but they were headed by group leaders who could not produce the expected results due partly to the excessive autonomy of the workers. In May 1969, Toyota carried out a review, and from 1971 the foremen became leaders of the QC circles under which mini-circles were formed with group leaders deciding on each theme or activity. In 1974, QC circles were reorganised with general foremen as leaders, and their themes were expanded from quality and operation improvements to cost, safety and maintenance. This decision facilitated rationalisation and the company's performance during the first oil crisis. But the QC circles led by general foremen were too big and inappropriate for the original aim of motivated, active involvement by workers. In the following year, when the world economy was beginning to recover and plant operations at Toyota had stabilised, QC circles were again reorganised. The form of the current QC circles was established at that time, with group leaders heading each circle and general foremen and foremen acting respectively as advisors or sub-advisors. More importantly, theme selection changed from a matter of company policy to a situation of free choice by circle members.[24] The organisation unit of QC circles, therefore, was frequently changed. Nevertheless, their number increased steadily (see Figure 1) and they functioned as support for the *Kanban* system. For example, the set-up time of pressing machines, central to smooth production and single unit output and conveyance, was reduced from one hour in 1971 to less than ten minutes in 1973 by rationalisation, procedural improvements, and the standardisation of operations as a result of QC work.[25]

FIGURE 1
HISTORY OF QUALITY CIRCLE ACTIVITIES

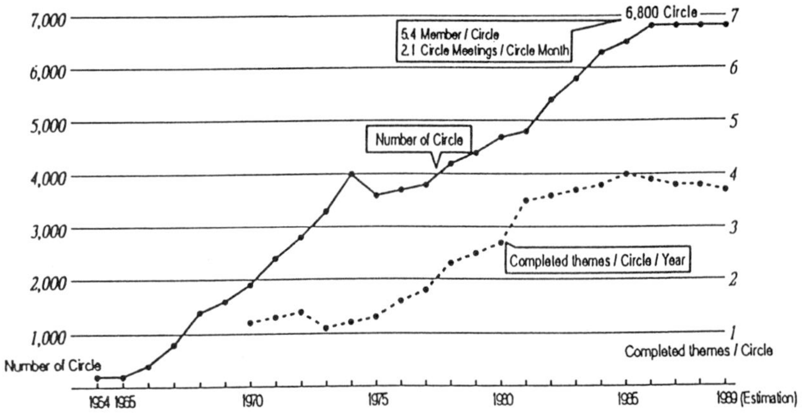

Source: Toyota Jidōsha Kabushiki Kaisha (Toyota Motor Corporation) (ed.), *QC Sākuru Katudō Nijugō-nen no Ayumi* (*Twenty-Five Years of QC Circle Activities*) (1989), p.79.

Toyota concentrated on fulfilling its slogan of 'All-Toyota Quality Assurance' by introducing TQC activities to affiliated companies, notably parts suppliers, as well as advocating *Kanban* to related concerns. In 1966, Toyota established a Purchasing Control Department, which assisted in the division of the primary components suppliers into three groups. The firm introduced a remuneration system of Value Analysis and Value Engineering, aiming to reduce the cost of parts used in the Corolla series. Fifty per cent of any proposed cost reduction achieved by a parts supplier was paid back. Also in 1966, Toyota started a process-reducing campaign in association with *Kyohokai*, and in the subsequent seminars the lessons of *Kanban* were also taught.[26] In 1968 and 1969, after a period of training provided for the primary parts suppliers, Toyota's Purchasing Control Department hosted a four-month course for the purchasing controllers of its suppliers. The aim was to create 'miniature Toyotas', which could in turn instruct the second- and third-tier suppliers. Toyota established a hierarchy amongst its parts suppliers in the early 1970s.[27]

At this time, the company encouraged its primary suppliers to apply for the Deming Prize, and in 1969 founded the Toyota Quality Control Prize for its second- and third-tier parts suppliers, the award acting as a quality control target and as a means of monitoring their operations.[28] In order to have an objective evaluation of its TQC activities, Toyota once more applied for the Deming Prize in 1970. It received an excellent assessment for improvement in QC work, and progress during the zero-defect campaign and the All-Toyota Quality Assurance System for the suppliers was acknowledged. The company was selected as the first recipient of the newly established Japan Quality Control Prize, and, soon afterwards, Toyota integrated its *Kanban* procedures and its concepts and methods into a unified Toyota Production System (See Figure 2).[29]

V

TOYOTA VERSUS NISSAN

Toyota consistently pursued its own development of passenger car technology. On the other hand, Nissan Motors benefited from technical co-operation with Austin in 1952, using its technology and production control methods. Until the early 1960s, its strategy of technical linkages was a success and the company obtained a reputation as 'Nissan of Technology' and 'Nissan of Exports'. Because of its success, it tried to expand its lead over Toyota and started construction of a modern mass production plant. It vigorously facilitated production automation and the computerisation of production control. Nissan selected this strategy against the *Kanban* system chosen by Toyota at that time. In the late 1960s, however, it became apparent to Nissan that the latest machines and computerised control of production could not bring about the necessary improvements in productivity, quality or the performance of products. In order to survive the first oil crisis, Nissan had to introduce its Action Plate System (APS), which was similar to Toyota's *Kanban*.[30]

FIGURE 2
OUTLINE OF TOYOTA PRODUCTION SYSTEM

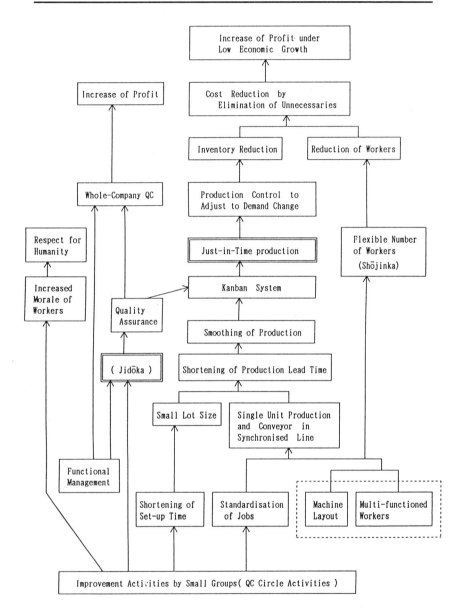

Source: T. Ohno and Y. Monden (eds.), *Toyota Seisanhōshiki no Shintenkai* (*New Development of Toyota Production System*), (Tokyo, 1983). p.236.

It had the advantage in quality control methods until the early 1960s. It introduced TQC activities in 1959 and won the Deming Prize in the following year, the first such occasion in the car industry. Because the company wanted the prize so badly, it forced its employees to participate in quality control training. As a result, they came to resent the QC programme. Top management also lost interest after the award had been gained, and gave priority to the construction of a modern mass production plant rather than quality control. According to Kaoru Ishikawa, Japan's leading expert on quality control issues, Nissan's QC programme changed in 1960 from the 'best' to only 'average'.[31]

Toyota's quality control activities were carried out very deliberately, over a long time-span, and in association with the *Kanban* system. In contrast to Nissan, it continued to regard TQC as the backbone of its management policy, even after winning the Deming Prize. Under the slogan of 'All-Toyota Quality Assurance', it pushed programmes for the reformation of supplier control and the vitalisation of QC circles. Nissan resumed its quality control activities in 1966, but it could not match Toyota's success, as it had a shortage of expertise. There was a lack of guidance for parts suppliers and its central Inspection Department continued to be too interfering and hierarchical.[32] Without a linkage with an overseas company, Toyota had to evolve its systems independently, and, without the resources and assistance available to Nissan, it had to rely on flexible methods and rapid set-up times rather than capital intensive long production runs. Its so-called lean system finally challenged the dominance of American or Fordist methods, allowing, thanks to quality control techniques, valuable savings in materials and defects. The car industry is one of Japan's most competitive industries and one of its highest export earners, and its success has been built upon the adoption of production management strategies developed during the 1950s and 1960s, implemented first by Toyota, and imitated later by Nissan.

NOTES

This study was financed in 1993 by the Special Research Subsidy Fund of Hosei University.

1. As a representative study, we can refer to J.P. Womack, D.T. Jones, and D. Roos, *The Machine that Changed the World* (New York, 1990).
2. Toyota Jidōsha Kabushiki Kaisha (Toyota Motor Corporation) (ed.), *Toyota Jidōsha Sanjūnen Shi* (*A Thirty-year History of Toyota Motors*) (Toyota City, 1967), p.333.
3. Ibid., p.347; E. Toyoda, *Watakushino Rirekisho: Ketsudan* (*My Personal History: Decision Making*), (Tokyo, 1985), p.148.
4. K. Sakakibara, 'Seisan Shisutemu niokeru Kakushin' (Innovation in the Production

System), in T. Itami, *et al.*, *Kyoso to Kakushin: Jidōsha Sangyō no Kigyō Seichō* (*Competition and Innovation: Corporate Growth in the Automobile Industry*) (Tokyo, 1988), pp.92–3; Toyota, *Thirty-Year History*, p.354.

5. In 1952 and 1953, technical tie-ups were concluded between Nissan Motors and Austin Motors of the UK, Hino Diesel Motors and Renault of France, Isuzu Motors and Rootes Motors of the UK, Shin Mitsubishi Heavy Industry and the Willys-Overland Export Corporation of the United States.

6. Toyota Jidōsha Kabushiki Kaisha (ed.), *Sozo Kagirinaku: Toyota Jidōsha Gojūnen Shi* (*Limitless Creation: A Fifty-Year History of Toyota Motors*), (Toyota City, 1987), p.248.

7. Toyota Jidōsha Kabushiki Kaisha (ed.), *Toyota Jidōsha Nijūnen Shi* (*A Twenty-Year History of Toyota Motors*), (Toyota City, 1958), pp.438–9.

8. M. Udagawa, 'Nihon Jidōsha Sangyō niokeru Hinshitsu Kanri Katsudo: Nissan to Toyota' (Quality Control Activities in the Japanese Automobile Industry: Nissan and Toyota), *Working Paper Series of the Center for Business and Industrial Research at Hosei University*, No.36 (September 1993), 21–2.

9. Toyota, *Limitless Creation*, p.332.

10. Ibid., p.332.

11. Nihon Jinbun Kagaku Gakkai (Japan Society of Human Science) (ed.), *Gijutsu Kakushin no Shakaiteki Eikyo* (*The Social Influence of Technological Innovation*), (Tokyo, 1963), p.58.

12. K. Wada, 'Jun Suichoku Togogata Soshiki no Keisei: Toyota no Jirei' (The Making of Quasi-Vertical Integration Type Organizations: A Case Study of Toyota), *Academia*, No.83 (Nanzan University, June 1984); Udagawa, 'Quality Control Activities', pp.21–2.

13. The import liberalisation of finished passenger cars took place in 1965 and international capital transfer in the automobile industry was liberalised after 1971.

14. Toyota, *Limitless Creation*, p.369.

15. T. Mizuno, 'Hinshitsu Kanri no Suishin to Sutafu no Yakuwari' (Quality Control and Staff's Role), *Hinshitu Kanri* (*Quality Control*), Vol.18 (Nov. 1967); Udagawa, 'Quality Control Activities', pp.23–4. The Deming Prize is the most prestigious award in quality control in Japan.

16. As to the details of the *Kanban* system, see T. Ohno, *Toyota Production System*, (Cambridge, MA, 1988); Y. Monden, *Toyota Production System* (Norcross, Georgia, 1983).

17. Ohno, *Toyota Production*, pp.111–12; Toyota, *Limitless Creation*, p.332.

18. H. Shiomi, 'Kigyo Gurupe no Kanriteki Togo' (The Administrative Coordination of Industrial Groups in the Japanese Automobile Industry), *Oikonomika*, Vol.22 No.1 (Nagoya City University June, 1985), p.23.

19. Toyota Jidōsha Kabusiki Kaisha (ed.), *QC Sakuru Katsudō; Nijūgo-nen no Ayumi* (*The Twenty-Five Years of QC Circle Activities*), (Toyota City, 1989), p.26.

20. As to the details of the *Kyohokai* see K. Wada, 'The Development of Tiered Inter-Firm Relationships in the Automobile Industry: A Case Study of the Toyota Motor Corporation', *Japanese Yearbook on Business History*, Vol.8 (1991), p.26.

21. Ibid., p.36.

22. Udagawa, 'Quality Control Activities,' p.29.

23. Toyota, *Limitless Creation*, p.427.

24. Toyota, *QC Circle Activities*, p.27.

25. Toyota, *Limitless Creation*, p.586.

26. Wada, 'Tiered Inter-Firm Relationships', pp.42–3.

27. Ibid., pp.44–5; see also W.M. Fruin, *The Japanese Enterprise System* (London, 1992), Ch.7.

28. M. Nemoto 'Toyota Hinshitsu Konrishō no Seitei to Un'e ni tuite' (The Establishment and Management of the Toyota Quality Control Prize), *Hinshitsu Kanri* (*Quality Control*), Vol.29 No.3 (1978). 80 companies were awarded the Deming Prize during the years from 1951 to 1988, of which 17 were Toyota and the member companies of

Kyohokai. During this period, 30 companies were awarded the Small- and Medium-Sized Company Prize of Deming, including 14 of Toyota's parts suppliers.

29. Toyota, *Limitless Creation*, pp.530–31. The Toyota production system is, on the one hand, regarded as a new and innovative manufacturing system for automobiles which can replace the Ford system. On the other hand, there is a critical view that it causes the overworking of workers and forces on suppliers the excessive burden of managing the delivery of parts. On the latter view, see S. Kamata, *Japan in the Passing Lane: An Insider's Account of a Life in a Japanese Auto Factory* (New York, 1983).

30. M.A. Cusumano, *The Japanese Automobile Industry: Technology and Management at Nissan and Toyota* (Cambridge, MA, 1985), p.317.

31. Ibid., p.369.

32. For a comparison of production systems and quality control programmes between Toyota and Nissan, see Cusumano's *Japanese Automobile Industry*, Chs.5 and 6, and Udagawa's 'Quality Control Activities'.

Work Rules, Wages, and Single Status: The Shaping of the 'Japanese Employment System'

SHINJI SUGAYAMA
Tohoku Gakuin University

What are the defining characteristics of the 'Japanese employment system'? From an historical perspective, it is apparent that the popular view of the 'three pillars' which comprise the system – seniority-based wages, lifetime commitment, and enterprise unionism – is superficial and incomplete. Instead, one must focus on the kind of forces that interacted to shape the unique *system* of employment relations in Japan, and on the process by which the system's various features eventually melded together. Ronald Dore's study *British Factory – Japanese Factory* remains a suggestive starting point for considering the evolution of employment relations in Japan. He stresses the increasingly widespread desire for social equality among industrial workers as an important factor in the formation of the Japanese system. According to Dore, the Japanese system 'differs from the British chiefly in that it accords to manual workers those privileges – fringe benefits like pensions and sick pay, considerable security of tenure, a rising curve of earnings constant with the increase in family responsibilities – which in Britain are restricted to middle class workers, and almost entirely denied to those who work with their hands'; although, as he is careful to point out, Japanese white collar workers also differed from their British counterparts in being less mobile and more organisation-oriented.[1] Kazuo Koike has published a detailed comparative study which supports Dore's arguments, offering cross-national data on age–wage profiles and length of service to demonstrate convincingly the similarities between Japanese blue-collar workers and white-collar employees in Western firms.[2]

When, how, and why did 'white-collarisation' of the Japanese industrial workforce take place? As discussed elsewhere,[3] an examination of the careers of skilled workers in modern Japan reveals that distinct, trade-based social groups of such workers did exist, but that the internal regulation of these groups was generally weak and that inflows of unskilled workers into their trades were not infrequent. Moreover, worker transfers – including those to other trades not closely related to prior occupational experience – were common at large Japanese factories before the Second World War. In general, Japanese blue-collar workers were characterised by a lack of strong allegiance to 'trade' or 'skill', a low social status only marginally above that of the working poor (*kasō-shakai*), and a strong desire for social respectability and advancement. In the West, on the other hand, groups of skilled workers often attained a relatively high and stable status in society by developing exclusive trade-based organisations with strong internal discipline. Significantly, Japanese white-collar employees, like workers on the shop floor, did not form any defined occupational groups with their own specific status cultures. The qualifications for white-collar employment were provided by a wide variety of educational programmes and institutions that around 1900 were open to persons from all social backgrounds, and academic credentials were used in due time as the main criterion for selecting business staff personnel.

It is not surprising that the Japanese labour movement sought the elevation of worker status rather than the extension of class consciousness, and that staff employees – treated by the company as 'regular' members of the enterprise community – constituted a 'reference group' and a model for workers' aspirations. Since the First World War, the Japanese labour movement has pressed for the principle of *jinkaku-sonchō* ('respect as human beings'), a slogan best interpreted as a demand for equal treatment between shop-floor workers and white-collar employees. Under union pressure, the managements of large companies introduced a variety of welfare programmes such as regular hiring combined with intra-company training, annual or semi-annual pay raises, and pension funds. Some managers, proclaiming that *shokkō* (manual workers) and *yaku-in* (white-collar staff) should constitute a harmonious whole, proposed a new single-status system of *jūgyō-in* (employees) and introduced factory councils that were intended as alternatives to labour unions.[4] Nonetheless, sharp status distinctions still existed in Japanese factories during the inter-war years. This essay seeks to explore how the established status order collapsed during the tumultuous years of total war and as a result of democratisation under the post-war American occupation. To illustrate the details of this process at the factory level, we will look at the changes in the specific work rules and wage systems. Special reference will be made to Hitachi Electric's Hitachi Plant, the very subject of Dore's study. The final section will offer an account of developments in the 1950s, and discuss the introduction of the regular hiring of blue-collar workers, a practice which constituted the finishing touch to the establishment of the 'Japanese employment system'.

II

EMPLOYMENT RELATIONS IN THE INTER-WAR YEARS[5]

Hitachi Electric, which was originally an electrical machinery repair shop attached to the Hitachi Mine of Kuhara Mining, achieved complete independence and became a limited company in 1920. In due course, the firm established basic work rules and wage regulations that would remain unchanged in principle up to 1939, despite frequent minor revisions.[6] The rules and regulations consisted of two parallel but separate codes – one for *sha-in* (white-collar staff) and the other for *shokkō* (manual workers) – and the basis for differentiated treatment of employees depending on their status within the enterprise was created.

Let us begin with the employment conditions of white-collar employees during the mid-1930s. According to the *Shain Tokyū oyobi Hōkyū Rei* ('ordinance on ranks and wages of white-collar employees'), *sha-in* were subdivided into an upper statum of *shoku-in* and a lower stratum of *ko-in*. There was also a separate category of *kenshūsei* (apprentices) in training to become *sha-in*. These trainees were youths of up to 20 years of age who would normally be promoted to *ko-in* after completing a two-year apprenticeship.

The single most important criterion in hiring white-collar employees was academic credentials; graduation from a university or a technical (commercial) higher school was expected for appointment as *sha-in*, and graduation from a vocational school was required for employment as *kenshūsei* or *ko-in*. The firm obtained the vast majority of new recruits from fresh school leavers who had the recommendation of their institution's principal, academic advisor, or its employment section, and who had passed the entrance examinations administered in March and April of every year. By the 1930s, most major companies and banks had established the practice of regular hiring upon graduation, and many firms had come to be closely linked with particular institutions of higher education and secondary schools throughout the country.[7] At Hitachi, graduates of post-secondary institutions formed 98 per cent of all those hired as *sha-in* between 1932 and 1938, with new graduates making up 77 per cent of the total. Graduates of vocational schools comprised 85 per cent of the *kenshūsei* and *ko-in* hired in the same period, with new graduates constituting 70 per cent of those employed in these categories.

With regard to remuneration, most white-collar employees were paid a monthly salary. They also received a twice-yearly bonus, the total of which amounted, on average, to 12 months' salary. Blue-collar workers, meanwhile, were given bonuses which added up, at most, to only two weeks' pay. The wage regulations prescribed the starting salaries of newly hired employees, the amount depending on academic credentials, and a regular pay raise with a merit component was annually available. An examination of salary data for all white-collar employees in 1936 reveals two interesting points. First, salaries tended to rise sharply and uniformly during tenure with the firm, employees with 20 to 24 years' service receiving a wage of almost three times the annual salary of employees with fewer than four years' experience. Second, and more pertinently, if we consider employees with the same graduation year according to educational institution attended (university, industrial higher school, and vocational school), hardly any had experience in other companies and consequently received pay higher than the average sum of those recruited directly from school. White-collar workers had little financial incentive to change jobs and were strongly induced by the wage system to stay with one firm. The turnover rate of white-collar employees dropped dramatically in the late 1920s – when the practice of regular hiring became firmly entrenched at Hitachi – falling to a level of around three per cent per year. The retention rate of white-collar staff employed in the late 1920s is estimated to have been about 70 per cent for graduates of vocational schools and 90 per cent for graduates of higher educational institutions.

While regular hiring, seniority wages, and lifetime commitment characterised the employment relations of white-collar employees, those of blue-collar workers were far from being comparably systematised. Those hired directly upon graduation to become apprentices at the Hitachi Company Industrial Training School comprised only seven per cent of all male regular workers recruited between 1932 and 1938. Moreover, there was a considerable number of temporary workers, which amounted to about half the total of regular workers in the mid-1930s.[8] Most of these seem to have been probationary employees, since a document dated 21 August 1936 reveals that it was a common practice at Hitachi to hire all manual workers (except apprentices) as 'temporaries', to be promoted to a regular position within a year or so.[9] The turnover rate of regular workers was around ten per cent per year between 1932 and 1936, although the figure doubled in 1937 and 1938. It is apparent, nevertheless, that if we take the large pool of 'temporary' workers into consideration, worker mobility was actually much greater than is suggested by these figures.

The company set a target daily wage for each blue-collar worker as the basis for determining individual payment rates. The company wage regulations prescribed the starting pay of inexperienced new employees, and provided for twice-yearly wage increases based on a merit system. On the surface at least, these practices looked much like those applied to the white-collar staff, but they did differ in some important respects. Firstly, unlike salaried staff employees, blue-collar workers could not expect regular wage rises. Pay increases were given selectively, and the criteria applied were obscure and inconsistent, decisions on merit raises usually being entrusted to individual foremen or staff personnel at the worksite. The writings of workers in labour union periodicals give us an indication of just how arbitrary and how vulnerable to abuse the remuneration system was.[10] Needless to say, under these arrangements, the daily wages of shopfloor workers did not necessarily rise with seniority. According to a study of the wage structure at Mitsubishi Nagasaki and Kobe Shipyard,[11] the wage curve of the average common worker levelled off after 13 to 14 years of service, and began to decline after 18 years. While those with no prior work experience were paid almost the same when hired, irrespective of their age, the starting wage of experienced workers were generally set somewhere between the average sum of common labourers and that of foremen of the same age cohort.

Secondly, those paid a daily wage amounted to only a portion of the total workforce, and the rest received payment by piece-rate. At Hitachi, time and motion study using a stopwatch was initiated in 1919, and standard operations and uniform pay rates were more or less established by 1925. This does not necessarily mean, however, that workers under the piece-work system were paid according to the jobs they actually performed. At Hitachi, as at other plants, it was common practice to undertake tasks in small groups, and in such cases payment was distributed to each worker based on his daily wage rate and the actual number of hours worked. Only the sub-foreman was paid a true day wage, but he also received an extra premium on his own and his subordinates' attendance rates.[12]

As can be deduced from the above accounts, the actual pay of a piece-rate worker belonging to a small group depended on the efficiency of the group as a whole and the breakdown of the members' daily wages, as well as on the worker's own daily wage and the number of hours worked. The financial incentives for diligent labour were not particularly strong under this system. The work rules for *Shokkō Shūgyō Kisoku*, which were full of minute and meddlesome prohibitions and detailed punitive regulations, suggest that, in motivating shopfloor workers, the 'stick' was more commonly used than the 'carrot'. The work rules present a picture of everyday factory life in the inter-war years that is characterised by worker laxity, strict surveillance by company guards and authoritarian behaviour by the white-collar staff. A worker was not allowed, for example, to leave his place even during a rest period; he was liable to be fined if he interfered with the work of other operations, if he sang, spoke loudly or cursed, and if he climbed over walls. Workers could have their daily wages docked when they made or repaired private belongings, and when they polluted water for drinking or factory use. Workers were subject to dismissal if they incited opposition to the company, when they stole something from the work-place, and even when they tore an official notice. Company guards closely watched the workers' gates, which were separate from those of the staff, and they refused admittance to all that arrived late or inebri-ated. The guards could also search a worker's body and his belongings anywhere and at anytime if they thought it necessary. Management's deeply rooted and entirely scornful preconceptions of the moral stan-dards of manual labourers lay at the heart of these intricate and explicit regulations for blue-collar workers. For white-collar employees, what corresponded to these work rules – *Fukumu oyobi Shōbatsu Rei* (disci-plinary ordinances) and *Kinmu Kisoku* (service regulations) – were writ-ten in a strikingly different manner. Only four items were specified as warranting punishment, one of which was behaviour considered degrad-ing to the reputation of the company staff. This disparity in corporate regulations between white- and blue-collar employees reveals that the proclamation of 'respect as human beings' and the establishment of a single status of *jūgyō-in* were mere lip service by the company management.

Another important aspect of status discrimination within the firm was the great income differentials between employment strata. According to an estimate based on data from Hitachi, the average yearly income (including bonuses and housing allowances) of staff employees in their late twenties who had graduated from university was 3.5 times that of shopfloor workers in the same age bracket. This differential expanded sharply to 3.7 times for employees 30–34 years old, 4.3 times for those 35–39, and to 6.1 times for workers aged 40–44. The average vocational school graduate was paid 1.7 times as much in his late twenties as the average blue-collar worker, and the wage disparity tended to broaden considerably over time, becoming 2.2 times for the 30–34 year-old cohort, 2.8 times for ages 35–39, and 3.4 times for 40–44 years. Income differentials were closely related to differences in living conditions, which were reflected most visibly in the employees' residential arrange-ments, especially in a company town like Hitachi. Houses supplied to staff employees by the company were called *yaku-taku*, and were spa-tially separated from the residences occupied by blue-collar workers.

The disparity in housing conditions was apparent, too, in the size of housing allowances given to those without company accommodation: the wage regulations specified the allowance to be 21 yen per month for a standard staff employee earning a salary of between 50 and 80 yen, as compared to three yen per month for a common manual labourer.

Finally, the job security of shopfloor workers has to be briefly considered. It is well known that mass dismissals were quite frequent in the inter-war years, and that in such instances elder workers with seniority were generally the most likely to be fired.[13] According to an estimate of employment adjustment speed (annual data, man-base) in the manufacturing sector in Japan, the average figure for the years between 1921 and 1935 was 0.98, as compared to 0.38 for the years between 1956 and 1970. In other words, it took only one year to adjust employment to an equilibrium level in the inter-war period.[14] At Hitachi, mass dismissals took place in 1930 and 1931, and 29 per cent of the total workforce on the company books at the end of 1929 were eventually fired. The proportion dismissed differed considerably by employment status, however. The figure for male regular workers was 36 per cent, as compared to only 12 per cent for staff employees who had graduated from a vocational school or higher institution. Although we must avoid drawing hasty conclusions from this data, the evidence clearly reveals status differentials within the firm.

III

THE IMPACT OF THE WARTIME PLANNED ECONOMY

In 1939, *shokkō*, the title officially given to the blue-collar worker stratum at Hitachi, was changed to *ko-in*, a term which used the same Chinese character, *in* (member), as the case of *sha-in*, the title applied to the white-collar status. Within a few years, there followed a series of revisions in the company's work rules, more equal treatment being granted to all employees on leaves of absence for funerals, consecutive holidays, and wedding vacations. Also in 1939, the plant manager at Hitachi set up a new advisory committee on wages, soon after the Wage Control Ordinance was promulgated. This ordinance was merely the first step in the government's efforts to extend full wage control over Japanese industry. A series of official pronouncements over the subsequent years – the Temporary Measures on Wages and Temporary Measures on Staff Salaries under the Wage Stop Order (1939), the Revised Wage Control Ordinance (1940), and the Corporate Accounting Control Ordinance (1940) – forced the committee repeatedly to revise Hitachi's wage regulations, and drove reform of the piece-work system. Finally, the enactment of the Ordinance on Labour Management in Essential Industries (1942), which required designated plants to submit work rules and wage regulations to the Welfare Ministry for approval, led to the establishment of completely new employment regulations at Hitachi in 1943. The new rules were based, for the most part, on the standard guidelines recommended in the ordinance.[15]

Behind such extensive government intervention in the management practices, of private companies lay a sense of rising discontent with the *laissez-faire* economic order and the spread of new ideologies of statist planning, especially in the bureaucracy and the intellectual community.[16] The 'New Economic Structure' movement of the Konoe Cabinet was of particular importance. Drawing on the model of Soviet Russia, the government's Cabinet Planning Board drafted an ambitious blueprint for systematic reform, the 'Essential Policy on the Establishment of the New Economic Structure'. The gist of this plan was the creation of a *dirigiste* economic order, one organized hierarchically into three strata (the government, industrial associations, and individual enterprises) and managed by means of quantitative directives flowing from the top down.[17] After making some important revisions, the Cabinet authorised the plan in December 1940, and an Ordinance on Important Industry Associations was enacted the next year.

Of fundamental importance to the original draft plan was reform of the essentially *laissez-faire* nature of the enterprises that constituted the lowest stratum of the 'New Economic Structure'. The Cabinet Planning Board insisted that enterprises should be 'free from the control of capital based on the profit principle', and proposed some daring prescriptions to encourage 'the separation of management and ownership', such as revision of the Commercial Code and controls over dividends. The Board drew up plans for the establishment of a 'New Financial Structure' and a 'New Labour (*kinrō*) Structure' to reinforce the state's ambitious vision of enterprise reform. The latter initiative outlined a new ideology of labour and management and it exerted a far-reaching influence, not only on wartime labour policy, but also on the workers' perception of 'fairness' and the objectives of the post-war labour movement.[18]

In its original plan, the Cabinet Planning Board stressed that *kinrō* (labour) should not be conceived as a tool of capital accumulation or a means of private gain, but rather as a form of service to the state. *Kinrō* was accordingly endowed with 'honour, as well as responsibility to the nation of the Emperor' and was considered a 'manifestation of humanity' (*zen jinkaku no hatsuro*). It was no coincidence that the pre-war labour movement, which had aimed at the elevation of the status of workers, had used the slogan of 'respect as human beings' (*jinkaku no sonchō*). The connotations of the 'New Labour Structure' ideology were apparent: all labouring men (*kinrō-sha*) could enjoy a respectable position both within the enterprise and, in turn, in the national community as well.

A crucial point is that the Cabinet Planning Board's scheme identified *kinrō-sha* with *seisan-jin* (persons who took part in production, including managers and staff personnel), and claimed the 'superiority of a substantive management body over an enterprise predominated by capital' or stockholder control. The fundamental policy of the plan was to 'make all *seisan-jin* unite and co-operate according to each person's *shoku-bun* (function) *without regard to differences in status position*' (author's italics). Toward that end, the Board outlined in its plan a new form of labour organisation, one which allowed for management participation and whose membership was open to the entire 'production management body', that is to managers, engineers and clerical personnel, as well as working hands. We can safely conclude that the original plan aimed to transform a private company into a 'production' community belonging to all labouring men or *seisan-jin*, in which all employees would be differentiated only by function and not by status.

Business leaders stubbornly resisted the 'separation of management and ownership' and, as a consequence, the 'Essential Policy on the Establishment of a New Economic Structure', the plan ultimately authorised by the Cabinet, simply defined the enterprise as 'an organic whole of capital, management, and labour'. While the basic attitude toward *kinrō* elaborated in the Cabinet Planning Board draft plan remained almost intact in the authorised 'New Labour Structure' policy, certain expressions crucial to enterprise reform such as *seisan-jin* and 'without regard to differences in status position' were deliberately eliminated. Nonetheless, structural changes in corporate governance did occur as a result of financial reforms, and the position of stockholders in management decreased considerably after 1941.[19] Labour management practices in private industry were also transformed, although this process was characterised by a regime of government intervention and direct control which went so far as to deprive managers of autonomy in the setting of basic work rules and wage regulations. This was, of course, the case at Hitachi.

The impact of the new official labour ideology was far-reaching indeed, especially on wage control policy. Literally speaking, since labour was considered service to the state, it was the responsibility of all workers to perform their jobs as efficiently as possible in order to fulfil their duty to the nation. Incentive wages were therefore inappropriate, as a financial 'carrot' was presumably unnecessary. Wages had to be worthy of the 'honour of the nation', and had to guarantee a decent and secure living to workers and their families. This idea of 'livelihood wages' was pursued all the more vigorously considering the sharp drop in real wages that was the grim reality of wartime Japan. The model wage rules provided by the Welfare Ministry specified the starting daily wages of *all* workers, with variations depending on sex, age, and years of experience. Various supplements, including family allowances, were prescribed, and a minimum wage was thus guaranteed to each worker, the minimum level rising with age and family responsibilities. Another model regulation stipulated that pay raises be given twice a year, and that all workers be eligible. Importantly, standards for maximum, minimum, and average raises were specified, the model rules recommending that the average should be at least five per cent of the mean daily wage. The Welfare Ministry's strict enforcement of these guidelines struck a serious blow to the arbitrary wage increase practices that had been so common in the inter-war years.[20]

The Ministry intended to 'rationalise' incentive wages in furtherance of its *kinrō* ideology. Ministry guidelines required that minimum, guaranteed levels of pay and standard methods of calculating unit prices and standard job times be stated formally in wage regulations. While available company data reveal a continuous and substantial increase in output pay over the course of the war,[21] some companies actually attempted to reform output payment schemes in such a way as to increase the stability of piece-workers' earnings. Hitachi, for example, adopted a time-rate work system instead of the former piece-rate in 1940, and established standard job times and individual time rates which corresponded to daily wages. Interestingly enough, prior to determining the correlation between time-rate and daily wage, staff personnel studied the relationship among age, income, and efficiency, and demonstrated that workers between 16 and 20 years of age and those over 36 years old should earn less than would have been expected. Another important reform was introduced in 1943, when a part of each piece-worker's wage packet was guaranteed, the proportion being a product of the daily wage rate and actual hours worked. According to data collected just prior to the end of the war, the breakdown of the average monthly income of time-rate workers at Hitachi was 108.54 yen in guaranteed wages, 67.29 yen in incentive payments, and 20.20 yen in various allowances, the total amounting to 196.03 yen.[22] The wage system at Hitachi was almost identical with the 'Guidelines for the Wages of *kinrō-sha* (*kō-in*)' adopted by the Welfare Ministry in the closing days of the war. The chief provisions of the government guidelines were as follows: (1) wages were to be composed of a base payment, a merit component, sundry allowances, and a bonus; (2) base wages were to be fixed, the levels determined principally on the basis of age, although length of service, rank, and skill were also considered. Payment was to be made monthly, but in case of unexcused absences wages were to be reduced for the days missed; (3) merit wages were to correspond to workers' individual performances and comprise, in general, about 30 per cent of the base wage.[23] It is remarkable that the guidelines were quite similar in basic outline to the famous Densan-style wages later demanded by post-war labour unions.

While 'white-collarisation' of workers' wages thus proceeded considerably during the war, the status order within Japanese enterprises was less affected by wartime reformism. The Welfare Ministry made two separate sets of model work rules, one for *kō-in* and the other for *shoku-in*, the latter explicitly identifying a staff employee as a leader within the firm. In the final analysis, the government differentiated *kinrō-sha* by hierarchical rank or status position, and not by function, as proclaimed in the draft plan of the 'New Labour Structure'. Some progress was indicated, however, by the fact that the two sets of work standards were virtually identical in form, the titles and chapters of the staff's rules essentially paralleling those of the workers' regulations. The disciplinary provisions for workers were quite simple, and punishment was much more lenient than that prescribed in the Hitachi code noted earlier. The model rules for workers proposed by the Welfare Ministry were not that different in form or in disciplinary philosophy from Hitachi's *post-war* work regulations, which were applied to all employees and which were established under labour union pressure. The government was not, however, as assertive in impressing its model work rules upon employers as it was in enforcing wage regulations.[24] Hitachi's new work regulations of 1943 still stipulated minute, meddlesome prohibitions, and allowed for body checks by company guards. The revised regulations continued to contain a chapter of 'workers' duties', which did not appear in the government's model rules, although it specified many fewer items for punishment than former company codes.

As the war intensified, the quality and morale of the changing labour force – and especially of drafted workers – declined sharply. In an attempt to compensate for this decay, the state and industry resorted to militaristic discipline and empty spiritualism as a means of revitalising Japanese production. The gap between ideology and reality was unbridgeable, and it seems that the workers' desire for change was steadily, silently mounting over the course of the war. Yet the desire of Japanese labour to have a decisive voice in enterprise reform had to lie dormant until the American occupation, when finally the flag of 'democracy' could be raised to its then highest point.

IV

'EMPLOYEE UNIONS' AND THE SEARCH FOR SINGLE-STATUS EMPLOYMENT

In August 1947, intensive research was carried out for the first time on the post-war labour union movement which had, after starting from zero, come to organise about five million people or more than 40 per cent of the total work force within the year and a half following Japan's surrender.[25] The results were sensational for those who expected the Japanese labour unions to follow the Western experience. The study revealed that almost all the unions surveyed were organised by enterprise, and that more than 80 per cent of them were so-called *kongō kumiai* (mixed unions) of white-collar employees and manual workers. In most cases, union membership was open to those generally considered to be managerial staff, including foremen, head clerks, and, in one-third of the unions, even section chiefs. Japan's post-war unions were clearly *jūgyō-in kumiai* ('employee unions'), and this label was adopted by some organisations rather than the term 'labour union' to describe themselves.

What accounts for the emergence of 'employee unions'? Union responses to the 1947 survey, which asked why mixed unionism was adopted, provide important clues. The most common reply was that white-collar staff and blue-collar workers were both equally employees, and that no substantial difference existed between the two groups. The distinction, if any, was only in *shoku-nō* (function); that is to say, in the different way each contributed to the process of production. The author of the survey explained simply that 'the concept of the mixed union can be interpreted as being related to practical aims such as the abolition of the status order, the democratisation of the enterprise, the adoption of a monthly salary system, and worker participation in management', and that 'the mixed union is regarded ideally as an organisation engaged in the struggle to win these aims and drive them home'. It is worth noting that several unions gave the answer 'for the purpose of reviving industry'. Because capital had been sluggish in resuscitating Japanese production after the war, employees, including staff personnel, organised unions in order to reform enterprises outside the control of capital, and thus further the rapid revival of the industrial economy.[26] It is not difficult to discern in this approach the profound legacy of the wartime ideology which dictated that enterprises should be 'production communities' dedicated to serving the nation.

The development of labour organisations at Hitachi provides a good example of the evolution of 'mixed unions' in occupied Japan. At Hitachi, blue-collar workers and white-collar employees were organised separately at the beginning in January 1946, but the two had merged into the Hitachi Plant Labour Union by May.[27] Interestingly enough, management believed that the establishment of the labour union was actually led by progressively minded white-collar employees, who persuaded leaders among the shopfloor workers to organise their own union.[28] The workers' organisation made its first demands only two weeks after its inception, and the document submitted to the plant manager is worth quoting at length to demonstrate what the workers sought, and more importantly, how they justified their demands:

> Our labour union is not a contentious organisation, but is founded on the belief that we should move beyond the existing capitalist order, encourage co-operation between management and labour through participation in management, create a system for making work interesting and involving, strive for industrial progress, and thus become the foundation stone on which the civilised nation of Japan may be established.
>
> But we must stop here and reflect. If labour is to move toward this goal, and attempt to contribute to the advance of industry, we must recognise first of all how important it is to improve working conditions. We cannot overestimate how significant it is to secure a minimum standard of living for the workers.
>
> How is a minimum standard of living to be guaranteed to the employees? Our experience indicates that the livelihoods of workers are not, at present, secure at all. . . . We are now facing a crisis in everyday life, and do not know what to do.
>
> Who dares to say there's no need to be afraid that these circumstances have led to the disappearance of the willingness to produce? We believe we are in the midst of a crisis of work which is, in turn, a crisis in the course of our nation.[29]

The union demanded a doubling of wages, the payment of cost of living allowances, and an enhancement of retirement benefit. Significantly, it also called for several democratic reforms, the most important being the complete revision of 'feudalistic' work rules and the abolition of discriminatory treatment such as special *yaku-taku* staff residences, housing allowance differentials, and body checks. The management reply to these demands was, however, far from satisfactory from the union standpoint. No actual steps were taken to revise the work rules, although some discriminatory policies were rescinded. On the matter of wage increases, the plant manager simply replied that he could not make a determination on the question by himself, and that the issue had to be considered on the level of overall company policy.

Lack of action prompted the establishment of the Hitachi General Federation of Labour Unions, a development which launched a new era in the history of labour relations at the firm. Joining the swell of labour activism that was sweeping the country, the General Federation pressed its wage demands and a general labour agreement as well. An agreement was signed in June 1946 and gave the union broad powers in corporate management, even allowing it a voice in personnel management decisions such as hirings, discharges, promotions, transfers, and temporary retirements. To facilitate involvement, its terms stipulated the creation of a Central Management Discussion Council as well as Factory Discussion Councils at each plant, and they emerged as instruments for, the 'democratisation' of company management. At the second meeting of the Central Management Council, held in October 1946, the General Federation demanded new work regulations which would be equally applied to both white-collar staff and shopfloor workers. Management was unable to present any reasonable objections and a plan drafted by the General Federation was authorised virtually without revision. The new code stated that 'An employee should not suffer from any status discrimination in his occupational career based on his academic achievement, age, sex, rank, etc.' (Article II), and that 'a superior should always show *respect* to his subordinates *as human beings*, and perform his duties in a democratic manner' (Article IV, author's italics).

The acceptance of new work rules was merely the beginning of a transformation in factory life at Hitachi Electric. The following month, the General Federation made what became known as the 'Three Major Demands': the abolition of the status hierarchy, the granting of pay raises in order to assure a minimum wage, and the revision of the labour agreement. It fought for two and a half months with considerable success, although some later complained about compromises on the issue of wage rises. At the same time, the Congress of Industrial Unions (*Sanbetsu*), which had been established in August 1946 under the influence of the Communist Party, was gaining influence among the Hitachi labour unions, and most of them, including the Hitachi Plant Union, joined *Sanbetsu* in 1946 and 1947. The revised labour agreement demanded by the General Federation made it possible for the union to conclude an agreement with the company in the capacity of a branch of *Sanbetsu*. The new agreement encouraged further worker participation in management, especially in personnel matters, secured freedom of political activities for employees, and took a firm, explicit stand against dismissals.

The Hitachi management also agreed that the status distinction between *sha-in* and *kō-in* be abolished and that all the employees be classed as *sho-in*. A committee composed of management and labour representatives was charged with the task of executing the plan. The matter did not, however, prove easy to resolve. The most controversial issues were the equitable apportionment of employees into the new job categories, and the establishment of an appropriate wage system. Management supported worker classification by *shoku-nō* (function), and divided the functions into four categories: 'Manual' labour was split into direct or line and indirect or secondary operatives; 'Mental' labour into clerical work and planning. The General Federation simply divided all the employees between direct or line operators and the others 'by common sense'. Interestingly enough, the General Federation did not deny the importance of *shoku-nō* itself, nor did it raise any explicit objections to the division between manual labour and mental work. What it stubbornly opposed, however, was the specification of the 'planners' category, which was clearly analogous to the former privileged status of *shoku-in*. The General Federation admitted that it was logical to categorise employees by function, but only 'if they could be classified *scientifically* in the strict sense of the word'.[30] It is worth remembering that Japanese workers were not particularly concerned with the divide between manual labour and mental work, as that distinction did not appear real to them, but placed complete confidence in 'science', which was assumed to be democratic and contrary to the *status quo ante* of managerial feudalism.

To be sure, the Hitachi managers shared the workers' belief in science, and this common faith exerted considerable influence on the subsequent course of events. In May 1947, the management and the General Federation concluded an agreement which provided for a new, uniform wage system based on a single status of employees. The chief points of the agreement were as follows: (1) wages were to be composed of base wages, additional payments, and various allowances; (2) the base wage was to be fixed, and paid as a monthly salary; (3) additional payments were to be made to direct or line operators based on the jobs they performed and were to comprise 45 per cent of the base wage; supplementary payments to indirect operators were to be determined by merit ratings, attendance rates and other elements, and were to comprise 30 per cent of the base wage. Significantly, the new base wage rates were correlated with the ages of the employees – naturally more advantageous to lower paid workers[31] – and, at a stroke, wage differentials between the former *sha-in* and *kō-in* became almost non-existent. According to survey data from August 1947,[32] an Hitachi Electric white-collar worker, who had graduated from industrial higher school, was aged 31 with 8–9 years of service and had two dependants, theoretically earned 3,252 yen per month, while a blue-collar worker, aged 31 with 12–13 years of service and with two dependants, had a theoretical monthly income of 2,745 yen. These figures were approximately equivalent to the standard level of wages at the nine companies surveyed in the electrical machinery industry, although three of them paid on average a blue-collar worker better than a white-collar worker.

It appears clear that the model of Densan-style wages, articulated by *Sanbetsu* in its noted 'October Struggle' of 1946, strongly influenced the thinking of the Hitachi General Federation, and, in turn, affected the establishment of the new wage system mentioned. Nonetheless, in subsequent negotiations, the General Federation agreed to the introduction of a job-ranking system, which aimed to put an end to 'the feudalistic nature of wages set on an individual basis', and to establish the principle of 'equal wages for equal jobs' by ranking tasks through scientific research.[33] Endeavouring to 'adjust the job-ranking system imported directly from the United States to the actual conditions of the company',[34] Hitachi management and labour nearly reached an agreement in April 1948.[35] In the end, however, the plan was never realised. Discussions were broken off when the General Federation demanded the establishment of a minimum wage system which calculated living costs based on calorific needs – that being a hallmark of the Densan-style wage structure – and launched into battle with the company. Only after the Hitachi 'great strike' of 1950, which marked a major shift of initiative in labour relations to the management camp, were the issues of job classification and wage determination finally settled. The management concluded that it would be impossible to apply a job-ranking system to the company, and that base wages would have to continue to be set individually. Each employee's base rate would be adjusted annually through merit ratings based on divisions into planning, clerical work, indirect or secondary operation, direct or line operation, and special work such as security and medical services. Yet the management did not completely abandon the idea that wages should be paid in accordance with the job being performed. It consequently sought to increase the proportion of additional payments in the wage packet, setting the ratio at 110 per cent of the basic wages of a direct operator, over twice the former rate of 45 per cent.

The company's turn to incentive wages was not as successful as expected. Investigations carried out in June 1954 reported that additional wage payments were actually quite uniform and consistent, not varying far above or below a standard rate of 100 per cent, and that as a consequence the labour union was indifferent to them.[36] This view coincides completely with Dore's description of the situation in the late 1960s.[37] Moreover, the Hitachi case does not appear exceptional.[38] Despite the advocacy of incentive wages by the Federation of Japanese Employers' Associations (*Nikkeiren*), the proportion of workers paid under such schemes showed a sharp drop in the 1950s, falling from 46 per cent of the total in 1950 to only 17 per cent in 1965. According to a recent study, Japanese managers during this period turned to strict personnel allocation, instead of wage incentives, as their main means of eliciting diligence and dedication.[39] To do this, the so-called 'rights of management' had to be regained, and labour agreements giving the unions wide scope in managerial participation, notably in matters of personnel administration, had to be reformulated. These conditions – and thus the ascendance of management – could only be realised in the wake of severe conflicts with labour and the destruction of the *Sanbetsu* federation during the era of the Dodge Line.

V

CONCLUSION

In many ways, the course of labour relations in the Japan of the 1950s can be seen as an outgrowth of what transpired during the preceding years of 'democratisation' under the American Occupation. The General Council of Trade Unions of Japan (*Sōhyō*), which had originated as a group of anti-Communist democratic cells *(mindō)* within *Sanbetsu*, turned to the left as early as 1952, and launched an extensive political campaign against rearmament and the San Francisco peace treaty. It also sought a voice in shopfloor conditions, and for explicit, detailed labour agreements with management. 'Shopfloor Struggle' (*shokuba tōsō*), a strategy developed by some leading unions such as those at Hokutetsu, Nissan, and Miike, even rivalled the vitality and unprecedented achievements in management participation which the union movement had attained in the early post-war 'labour offensive'. What was new about the movement in the 1950s was that it focused on the regulation of the work process and who should control it, while regarding responsibility over personnel administration as one of the 'rights of management'.[40]

This new challenge to the authority of management in the 1950s disintegrated within a few years. By 1955, when the high-speed growth of the Japanese economy began in earnest, virtually all the activist unions (with the exception of that at Miike, which survived until 1960) had collapsed. In most cases, the contentious, politicised unions were replaced by the 'second unions' which sought to co-operate with the management, raise productivity, and share eventually in economic rewards. The famous spring labour offensive (shuntō), institutionalised during the era of rapid economic growth, can be seen as a mechanism which ensured that labour unions would receive due rewards. Co-operative unions came to be the norm at large companies in the private sector by about 1960, a situation which was a prerequisite for the construction of the system of continuous innovation and flexible work organisation which took place over the ensuing decade.

It took a relatively long time, however, for management to establish an independent wage policy which conformed to the distinctive conditions in Japan. Since frequent worker transfers were common under the flexible production system, it was apparent that wage rates had to be determined separately from the jobs actually being performed. Nonetheless, management as well as labour unions continued to look toward job-related payments throughout the 1950s, and Nikkeiren strongly supported functional wages based on 'scientific' job evaluations, even after it had abandoned efficiency wages. Once again, the application of a system imported from the West proved impractical, and, after ten years of trial and error, Nikkeiren finally and definitively rejected foreign wage models in the mid-1960s. Nikkeiren concluded that, in order to promote meritocracy within the enterprise, wages should be paid according to each person's job-performance abilities and be evaluated synthetically by merit-rating standards.[41]

Finally, the practice of regularly recruiting blue-collar workers from linked high schools,[42] a process formalised only in the 1960s, has to be briefly considered. Contrary to popular wisdom, the hiring practices of large factories in the 1950s were almost identical to those of the mid-1930s. Quantitatively speaking, those taken directly upon graduation from junior high school to company training institutions were only a fraction of total recruits. The majority of newly hired blue-collar workers came from the large pool of 'temporary workers', who, once judged to be useful, were promoted to regular positions in their firms.[43] What had a particularly great impact on this situation was the acute shortage of labour which followed rapid economic growth, and a remarkable improvement in academic achievement throughout Japan. The number of temporary workers fell sharply in the 1960s, and companies began to employ high school graduates – who formerly would have worked in low-level white-collar jobs – as manual labourers. This shift had significant effects on recruitment management, since the major companies had already established a system in which job vacancies were matched to available graduates by the employment services at affiliated high schools, these arrangements paralleling the relationships forged between companies and the former secondary schools during the inter-war years. It is likely that companies had no choice but to introduce regular hiring practices for blue-collar employees, as well as for white-collar staff, when they were forced to turn to high school graduates as their source of shopfloor workers. In this sense, the establishment of regular recruiting upon graduation can be interpreted as another instance of 'white-collarisation', although much research remains to be done to confirm such an analysis.

NOTES

1. R. Dore, *British Factory – Japanese Factory* (Berkeley, 1973) pp.264–5.
2. K. Koike, 'Internal Labor Markets: Workers in Large Firms', in T. Shirai (ed.), *Contemporary Industrial Relations in Japan* (Madison, WI, 1983).
3. S. Sugayama, 'Business Education, Training, and the Emergence of the "Japanese Employment System"', in N. Kawabe and E. Daito (eds.), *Education and Training in the Development of Modern Corporations* (Tokyo, 1993).
4. T. Hyōdō, *Nihon ni okeru Rōshi-kankei no Tenkai* (*The Evolution of Labour–Management Relations in Japan*) (Tokyo, 1971), Ch.3; Y. Nakanishi, 'Dai-ichi-ji Taisen Zengo no Rōshi-kankei' ('Labour–Management Relations Before and After World War I'), in M. Sumiya (ed.), *Nihon Rōshi-kankei Shiron* (*Historical Essays on Labour–Management Relations in Japan*) (Tokyo, 1977).
5. The analysis in this section is based primarily on S. Sugayama, 'Senkanki Koyō-kankei no Rōshoku-hikaku' ('The Interwar Employment System in Japan: A Comparative Study of the Employment Conditions of White-Collar Staff and Workers'), *Shakai Keizai Shigaku*, Vol.55 No.4 (1989); 'The Bureaucratization of Japanese Firms and Academic Credentialism: A Case of Hitachi Ltd', *Japanese Yearbook on Business History*, Vol.8 (1991).
6. Hitachi Kōjō, 'Hitachi Kōjō Gōjō Nenshi: Rōmu Kanri' ('Fifty Years of Hitachi Plant: Labour Management') (unpublished manuscript). The work rules and wage regulations on which this study is based are owned by the *Odaira Kinenkai* at Hitachi Plant and by Nakajō Plant Hitachi Ltd.
7. See, for example, Chūō Shokugyō-shōkai Jimukyoku, *Kaisha Ginkō Teiki-saiyō Jōkyō Chōsa* (*Research on the Regular Recruiting Practices of Companies and Banks*) (yearly).
8. Hitachi Kōjō, *Jigyō Hōkoku; Hitachi Kōjō* (*Business Report: Hitachi Plant*) (monthly).
9. H. Kitamura, 'Shokkō Idō ni Tsuite' ('On Worker Mobility').
10. A. Gordon, *The Evolution Labor Relation in Japan* (Cambridge, MA, 1988), Ch.5.
11. Hyōdō, *Labour–Management Relations*, pp.453–71.
12. Hitachi, *Labour Management*, pp.14, 15.
13. H. Hazama, *Nihon Rōmu-kanri-shi Kenkyu* (*Studies in the History of Japanese Labour Management*) (Tokyo, 1964), Ch.1
14. T. Okazaki, 'The Japanese Firm under the Wartime Planned Economy' in M. Aoki

and R. Pore (eds.), *The Japanese Firm* (Oxford (1994), pp.357–9.
15. Hitachi, *Labour Management*, Ch.3.
16. T. Nakamura and A. Hara, 'Keizai Shin Taisei' ('The New Economic Structure'), in Nihon Seiji Gakkai (ed.), *'Konoe Shintaisei' no Kenkū (A Study of the 'New Konoe Regime')* (Tokyo, 1972).
17. Okazaki, 'Wartime Planned Economy', pp.360–701.
18. K. Saguchi, *Nihon ni okeru Sangyō Minshushugi no Zentei (The Preconditions of Industrial Democracy in Japan)* (Tokyo, 1991), Part II, examines the *authorised policy* on the Establishment of the New Labour Structure. The original plan is included in *Mindoe Papers* (Collections of the Tokyo University Library) G–32–1.
19. Okazaki, 'Wartime Planned Economy', pp.367–73.
20. Shōwa Dōjinkai, *Waga Kuni Chingin-kōzō no Shiteki-kōsatsu (An Historical Analysis of the Wage Structure in Japan)* (Tokyo, 1960), Part II, Ch.4.
21. Gordon, *Labor Relations*, pp.281–4.
22. Hitachi Kōjō, *Labour Management*, pp.67–79.
23. Shōwa Dōjinkai, *Wage Structure*, pp.315–8.
24. Kōsei-shō Rōmu-kyoku, *Jūyō Jigyō-ba Rōmu-Kanri-rei Unyō-hōshin (Policy on the Application of the Ordinance on Labour Management in Essential Industries) (Tokyo, 1942)*, pp.1–8.
25. Tokyo Daigaku Shakaikagaku Kenkyūjo (ed.), Sengo Rōdō Kumiai no Jittai (The Conditions of Postwar Labour Unions) (Tokyo, 1950).
26. Ibid., Ch.3.
27. Hitachi Seisakusho Hitachi Kōjō Rōdō-kumiai, *Hitachi Rōdō Undō-shi (A History of the Labour Movement at Hitachi Plant)* (1964), pp.72–115. This source provides the basic information which underlies this section and will not hereafter be footnoted.
28. Hitachi Kōjō, 'Hitachi Kōjō Gojūnen-shi; Rōdō-undō-shi' ('Fifty Years of the Hitachi Plant; A History of the Labour Movement') (unpublished manuscript), p.2.
29. Hitachi Kōjō Rōdō-kumiai, *Labour Management*, p.84.
30. Hitachi Seisakusho Rōdō-kumiai Sōrengō, *Hitachi ni okeru Shokkai Seido no Keika (The Progress of the Job-ranking System at Hitachi Electric)* (1950), pp.1–35.
31. For further details, see Hitachi, *Labour Management*, pp.114–17.
32. Tokyo Shōkō-kyoku, *Kabushikigaisha Hitachi Seisakusho Chōsa Hōkoku-sho (A Research Report on Hitachi Ltd)* (1948), pp.21–4.
33. Sōrengō, *Job-ranking System*, pp.38–41.
34. Hitachi, *Labour Management*, p.94.
35. Sōrengō, *Job-ranking System*, pp.41–167.
36. Nihon Keieisha Dantai Renmei, *Nōritsu-kyū no Gendaiteki Kōsatsu (An Examination of Efficiency Wages)* (Tokyo, 1956), Appendix, p.39.
37. Dore, *British Factory*, pp.107–8.
38. K. Kōshiro, 'Dantai Kōshō to Nenkō Chingin' ('Collective Bargaining and Seniority Wages'), in M. Sumiya (ed.), *Sangyō to Rōdō-kumiai (Industry and Labour Unions)* (Tokyo, 1959) presents various examples.
39. M. Nitta, 'Nihon to Beikoku ni okeru Nōritsu-kanri no Tenkai' ('The Evolution of Efficiency Management in Japan and the United States'), in M. Ishida *et al.* (eds.), *Rōshi-kankei no Hikaku Kenkyū (Comparative Studies on Labour-Management Relations)* (Tokyo, 1992).
40. T. Hyōdō, 'Shokuba no Rōshi-kankei to Rōdō-kumiai' ('Labour-Management Relations on the Shopfloor and Labour Unions') in S. Shimizu (ed.), *Sengo Rōdō-kumiai Undō-shi-ron (Historical Essays on the Postwar Labour Union Movements)* (Tokyo, 1982).
41. M. Ishida, *Chingin no Shakaikagaku (Social Science on Wages)* (Tokyo, 1990), Ch.2.
42. Concerning specifically Japanese aspects of the linkage between enterprises and high schools, see T. Kariya, 'Institutional Networks Between Schools and Employers and Delegated Occupational Selection to Schools: A Sociological Study on the Transition from High School to Work in Japan' (unpublished Ph.D. thesis, Northwestern

University, 1988); *Gakkō, Shokugyō, Senbatsu no Shakaigaku* (*A Sociology of Schools, Occupations, and Selection*) (Tokyo, 1992) .

43. K. Yamamoto, 'Dai-kigyō Rōdōsha' ('Workers in Large Firms'), in S. Ujihara (ed.), *Kōza Rōdō-keizai 1: Nihon no Rōdō-shijō* (*Labour Economics Series 1: Labour Markets in Japan*) (Tokyo, 1967).